BULLIES PARASITES AND SLAVES

REPLACING EXPLOITATION WITH MUTUAL CARE

GEORGE BYRON KOCH

Finding Courage…

This book is a grueling, difficult and plain-spoken critique of our world's ongoing conflicts and conquests, and the political, economic and social systems that hurt us and those we love.

Followed, I believe, by a solution for us to move beyond them, together.

In our era of disdain, memes, misinformation and extreme partisanship, know this: there will be no favor shown here to any individual, party, sect, social or religious movement. This isn't the left, right or middle of anything. Instead, it looks directly at the devices and disguises that all bad leaders employ, the harm they commit… and *our response*.

Have we seen it yet? Have we excused it, or looked the other way?

Some who are partisans of any party or ideology will despise and deny what is disclosed here, will find their own character and methods exposed, and will surely hate that their cruelty is being called out.

But it must be faced: wisely and substantively. It is real, pervasive, and morally *wrong*.

Finally, we must find the courage to see it not just in our *foes*, but in *ourselves* and *our* heroes and leaders.

And then, together, we must *change it*.

ByronArts.com
PO Box 87260
Carol Stream, Illinois 60188-7260

Bullies, Parasites and Slaves

Copyright © 2025 by George Byron Koch. All rights reserved. Permission is granted to copy or reprint limited portions for noncommercial use or reviews. Initial limited release 2024 to critics and friends for critique, correction and counsel. General publication First Edition, July 2025.

ISBN13: 978-0-9777226-2-4
ISBN: 0-9777226-2-7

Sources, Methods, References and more: **BPS.online**

Credits and professional contact information:

Cover Design by Mir Imran Hossain
csoeht@gmail.com / **www.pexsit.com**

Copyediting and Layout by George August Koch
GeorgeAugustKoch@me.com / **www.CopyEdit.pro**

Author photograph by Steven Koch Photography, LLC.
hello@stevenmkoch.com / **www.StevenMKoch.com**

Website development by Bryan Hoffman
bryanhoffman1@gmail.com / **www.bryanhoffman.xyz**

The History of Byron Arts

This independent little company was established decades ago for a long indulgence of the author: a gallery for ancient and modern pottery, and for his technical writings and resources about both. He has a well-worn ceramics studio behind his garage.

The owner, George Byron Koch (*"coke"*), has been writing for even longer than he has been throwing clay. He has been widely and often published and heard, in several fields and over decades, in books, journals, magazines and newspapers, and in talks and teachings, since the mid-'60s. An extensive collection of his art, talks and writings, beyond what is available through Byron Arts, is at **GeorgeKoch.com**.

Some twenty years ago this online gallery evolved into a small publishing company, as a means to oversee his own work and that of other authors he knew and respected: in print, electronic form, online and on the air: **ByronArts.com** is the access site for this.

George's books have been published in eight languages around the world, and more than a million copies sold. One of them, *What We Believe and Why*, is heard daily on some 700 radio stations in the United States and beyond, and is now in more than 70 countries.

Bullies, Parasites and Slaves is the latest, tightly yoked to two sites with free resources: **BPS.online** and **MutualCare.online**.

Acknowledgments

People. It's always about people. Creating this book required the labor and abilities of many, and they are deeply appreciated.

George August Koch is a gifted writer and editor, insightful and intellectually rigorous. His edits sharpened every aspect of this book: accuracy, structure, tone and clarity. Again and again, he turned dense or muddled phrasing into prose that communicated with precision and force. This is his profession, and he excels at it. Many others have seen his talent. It's a privilege to call him my son, but he earned this role entirely on merit.

Reach him at **copyedit.pro** and **GeorgeAugustKoch@me.com**.

Mir Imran Hossain created the art and layout for the cover. He has the eye of an artist and the technical skills of a programmer. He understands quickly what is needed, and turns around design changes and updates quickly. I value and appreciate him.

Reach him at **pexsit.com** and **csoeht@gmail.com**.

Steven M. Koch, the author's nephew and a renowned portrait photographer, did the back-cover photo. He is gifted with a wonderful eye, does excellent composition, and is easy to work with.

Reach him at **StevenMKoch.com** and **hello@stevenmkoch.com**.

Angelo A. and the **WordPress.com** team created the beautiful websites for this book, **BPS.online** and **MutualCare.online**. They understood the purpose of the book and reflected it wonderfully in their creations.

Bryan Hoffman took the websites created by the WordPress team, and created their logic, simplicity and accessible form. The organization of the sources and links, the content and its usefulness, are due to Bryan's clear vision and dedication.

Reach him at **bryanhoffman.xyz** and **bryanhoffman1@gmail.com**.

Holly Holmberg did the extraordinary research for the sources that underpin this book and its premise, including histories, annual reports, organizations, religions, and more. When you find a reference in the text, or a link in **BPS.online** or **MutualCare.online**, it was almost certainly found and placed there by her. This book and its resources could not have come into existence without her gifted and unflagging efforts.

Several people spent time reading and critiquing early versions of this book, to help improve it and make it more effective and understandable. They include Denise, George, Jim, Joanna, Laura, Linda, Melanie, Morgan, Rebecca, Yudit and James. My thanks to them!

Lastly, my deep gratitude to my wife Victoria, and my sons George and Isaiah, for their unflagging support and encouragement over many years. They loved me and put up with me! And to our decades of rescue dogs—Specs, Blackie, Fred, Misty, Freddie and Efren—who became experts at love.

I couldn't have made it through without all of you.

Foreword

What follows is all about *each of us* seeing the mistaken, failed methods of human bullies and parasites—and the kinds of bad leadership and immoral values we've had imposed on us. They couldn't and didn't work. Many people were exploited to subsidize a few, and this unbalanced and ugly social order was dressed up as productive and necessary. It is neither.

Once we have seen and fully grasped why those old and evil methods fail to make us prosper and thrive, trapping us in wasteful combat, then we can begin to see and be taught, to be trained up, in the "how to" of replacing exploitation with mutual care: in our country, in our world, in our whole human family. Mutual care is, finally, the solution. Not just in some heady, moralizing theory, but in practical reality.

What qualifies me to pretend to coach anyone else about any of this? You can read my biography or research my experience if you wish, but I suspect the insights I've gained aren't unique. Many others, including you, have likely come to the same understandings. My contribution, perhaps, is in simply laying them out in an accessible form, one that might help others *not quite there yet* to look and see more fully—the whole jigsaw puzzle, complete—and then pass it on.

In the pages ahead I'll stay true to the facts and the science, using key examples from our long human history of mistakes and successes—showing *what to avoid*, *what to do*, readily condemning *immoral conduct*, and explaining *wiser* solutions that benefit *all of us*.

This will likely read more like a heart-to-heart than a text by an economist, political theorist or journalist. The theory and reporting will all be there, but grounded in lived examples—from my personal experiences and those of countless others throughout history.

We'll learn how to love and care for each other, with growing empathy for each other's needs, and the patient, willing care required to meet them. We'll learn how to identify and resist *exploitation*, and replace it with *mutual care* for each other.

Regardless of which political parties you belong to, which religions or philosophies inspire you, in the end we must all see that there is but one solution that meets all of our needs, and protects all of our rights: MUTUAL CARE. Let's make it our relentless moral code and method.

George Byron Koch

x

Table of Contents

PART 1: THE PROBLEM 1
Simply Put 3
   The Problem: Exploitation 3
   The Solution: Mutual Care 4
Proving the Claims 5
   What About the Rich? 5
   Defining Three Terms: Bullies, Parasites, Slaves 6
Discarding a Myth 9
Preparing to Act 11
Seeing Thieves 13
Bullies 15
   Toxic Mold That Threatens 15
   Seeing Them Where They Are 16
   Local Bullies: Protection Rackets and Approvals 23
   National and Worldwide: Bully Officials and Parasites 27
   Bullies in History 29
   Chicken Thieves and Nobles 36
   Judging History 37
   Bullies: In Conclusion 39
Parasites 41
   Begging 42
   Skimming Pennies, Paper and Accounts Payable 43
   Misdirection – *Look at That!* 45
   Extortion 47
   Conspiracy Isn't All Theory 48
   Embezzlement and Conversion 49
   Hiding in Plain Sight 50
   Grandpa, Princes and Rich Widows 50
   Distraction by Threat and Entertainment 52
   Conning the Marks 53
   Evil Laws 54
   Fear, Lies, Labels and Name-Calling 55
   Honorable Leaders 60
   Leaders Who Lie 61

Slaves	63
Upper Class	63
Middle Class	64
Lower Classes	64
Slaves in History	64
What Color Are Slaves?	65
Hidden Slaves Today – Retail Slavery	75
We Subsidize Them	77
What About Pay Differential?	78
Stuck in Poverty? I Don't Believe It.	78
Propaganda	83
Kinds of Lies	83
All the Places Propaganda Lives and Works	84
PART 2: THE SOLUTION	**93**
Overcoming Pride and Fear	95
Privilege	96
The Predatory Hierarchy	100
Banning the Slave Trade	101
Joining Care With Wisdom	103
The Loving of Wisdom	104
The Wisdom of Loving	105
The Golden Rule	107
A Reciprocal Call to Action	109
The Gold in the Gravel	110
Mother of Exiles	111
"That Black Man"	111
Turning Their Enemies Into Your Enemies	111
Immigrants	112
Illegal Aliens	113
Joining Rights and Obligations	117
For Each, From Each	118
Taxing Ourselves	121
Making Healthcare Mutual	123
The Evidence of Theft	123
What About Universal Healthcare?	125
The Logistics of Healthcare	128
Our Rights and Obligations	131
The History of Rights	131

- Representative Democracy 133
- Rights, With Obligations 134
- Mutual Care and Protection 135

The Way of Mutual Care 137
- Abundance and Liberty 139

Authority – Who Is in Charge? 141
- Forms of Authority 141
- Acknowledged – What the Expert Knows or Believes 142
- Imposed, Persistent and Ingrained 144
- Granted (Consented To or Accepted) 147
- The Model of Mutual Care 147

Upholding Democracy 149
- Two Ancient Economic Systems 150
  - o Hunter-Gatherer / Farming 150
  - o Feudalism 150
- Three New Economic Systems 150
  - o Socialism 150
  - o Communism 151
  - o Capitalism 151
- Economic Systems, Democracy and Mutual Care 152

How to Train Up True Leaders 155
- Supervision and Mutual Care 159

Coordinated Action 161

What You Can Do Now 163
- o Bullies and parasites 163
- o Slaves 163
- o Mutual Care 163
- o Our Evolutionary Imperative 164

About the Author 165
Glossary of Terms 167
Index 177

PART 1: THE PROBLEM

In a lifeboat large enough for everyone,
throwing others overboard
and hoarding provisions
does not prove
your worthiness to be captain.

It shows you should be in restraints.

SIMPLY PUT

We need a hard reset on who we are—and who we allow to lead us.

Bullies and *parasites* are those in our neighborhoods and nations who steal from others and reduce them to *slaves*. They *exploit* lives to subsidize their own.

This happens in dictatorship and democracy. In communism and capitalism. In government and industry. In our country and worldwide, *we all suffer* under the manipulations and abuses of bullies and parasites.

It is time for us to recognize it, confront it, and change it.

We can only create a thriving, abundant future for all by replacing *exploitation* with *mutual care*.

THE PROBLEM: EXPLOITATION

Bullies start in the neighborhood, but go on to rule gangs, businesses, cities, nations. They victimize for gain, causing loss, poverty, injury, even death. They steal, hoard and bind us by lies, laws and fear. They claim privilege by inheritance, power or divine right. For millennia, they've spent our lives not for the common good but to secure dominance—through conquest, control and exploitation. They waste resources that should be used to prosper us all.

An ancient slogan of conquerors and kings has been "FORCE AND WILL!"—which literally means hurting others to get what you want.

Bullies glorify this as *leadership*. They pose as protectors of life, family and prosperity. And we buy it. We elect or support them while they keep us bound through false promises and fear. Our work subsidizes them. We multiply their wealth and power through the loss of our own.

With few exceptions, this has been the human story. If we think this is hyperbole, hype or hopeless, then their deceptions are working.

The goal is urgent: to see how exploitation threatens not just others—but *us* and *those we love*. If we are blind to that danger, or indifferent, we guarantee misery for our children's futures and our own.

We can change it, if we truly see it.

THE SOLUTION: MUTUAL CARE

Against exploitation and self-glory, some have stood out—individuals and movements who fearlessly exposed our human failings and then pointed the way to a more abundant future—mutual care.

Mutual care brings thriving and abundance. It frees us from bullies' control. When we contribute our lives and resources to benefit each other—not them—we increase what's available to enrich us all. A simple truth with a good result.

Critics scoff: "Nice idea, but naïve. We tried it. It doesn't work."

That's true—for bullies and parasites. It *doesn't* work for them. Mutual care ends their theft, hoarding, cruelty and lies. That's the only sense in which mutual care "doesn't work."

So they try to frighten us away from trying it, or shame us as fools.

But for the rest of us, mutual care *works*. It brings us thriving and abundance. It's wise, right and imperative: do it—or stay in servitude.

It is truly this simple: Protect each other's rights, meet each other's needs. *True leadership* does exactly this. We thrive when we *help each other* thrive. Together we create and share abundance.

We can choose that—but first we must *fully understand* where and how bullies and parasites steal abundance—by stealing from us. That is the first half of this book: exposing the methods of their serial thefts and murders. A wrenching discovery—but necessary for our futures.

We are not predestined to their control. It is neither inevitable nor eternal. But it is where we are now. The sooner we see it, the sooner we free ourselves from it—and our children—and all the generations ahead.

Ironically, the most perfectly selfish thing you can do to ensure care and thriving for yourself and those you love… is to ensure it for all.

When mutual care replaces exploitation, abundance stays with those who make it—you and me. We protect each other. We help each other thrive.

The practical "how" of leadership and vision is the focus of the second half of this book: where no one is exploited, excluded or left behind.

It is right, fair, and wise. And it is time.

That's what this *whole* book is about.

PROVING THE CLAIMS

There's little value in simply making a claim that we are slaves in a system that benefits bullies and parasites, or that their lies help keep us in our place. Anyone can make a claim of victimhood, and false claims make us wary even of true claims that face us.

I have to prove it, to show how it works, so I'll give illustrations from ancient history to today, from our own neighborhoods to across the world. I'll link my sources and methods, show my work and calculations and give resources and expanded topics at **BPS.online**, where you can research and substantiate it for yourself. This QR code will take you there:

Anything I condemn or commend will be established by substantive evidence, chapter by chapter and claim by claim. An online version of this book will contain those supports with direct links to the evidence. You can see them also, by chapter and topic, by going to **BPS.online** and looking under *Sources*. I invite you to look rigorously, and if you find it compelling, to take it further yourself, and even contribute to the site. You can and should be a part of the solution.

WHAT ABOUT THE RICH?
Importantly: This is not a diatribe against just anyone with wealth, power or influence. There are people with all of these whose lives and fortunes are actively shared for the care of others, whose hearts are led by empathy, not condescension. They are relentlessly thoughtful, kind and compassionate, and use their positions to help directly those in need—and to change the circumstances, laws and leaders that have kept them down.

Nor do I disparage those whose hard work, investment and innovation have lifted them up economically or socially. They may use what they have created to lift others as well, and many of them do just exactly that, creatively and intentionally. Some have built medical facilities, funded research, and given of their time, brilliance and assets to help those in need. Others have invested heavily in new technologies that will help in medicine, food, shelter, education, logistics and more.

I have had the privilege to know such people. You know who you are.

Still others, who have little or no wealth, give their lives helping those in need. I have had the privilege to know many of these as well.

All of these people deserve our honor and thanksgiving. *Thank you.* It gives me joy to know that you exist.

For those who steal and hoard, however: The problem isn't striving to achieve; it is using *theft* to achieve. So the goal ahead is a careful and systematic unveiling of theft by those who exploit others, who steal and hoard—of who they are and *how they do it*. The more we are all aware of their devices and disguises, and the social, political and economic systems they are able to manipulate, the more we can strive to free ourselves from their exploitation.

We will use this freedom to care for each other instead. It isn't enough just to be able to see a problem and identify its roots. We need to know how to *solve* it. Part 2 of this book will provide detail and logic for a substantive and evolving *solution* that we can create *together*.

I'll provide growing resources for that as well, at **MutualCare.online**. This QR code will take you there:

The two sites are tightly linked and free.

DEFINING THREE TERMS: BULLIES, PARASITES, SLAVES

Let's begin by carefully defining three terms, to give us consistent and common language when facing down the predators before us:

- **Bullies** *take because they can.* They *steal openly* with intimidation, physical harm and even murder in their predation, if needed. They include conquerors, monarchs, autocrats, gangsters, corrupt officials, and the student who steals your lunch money at school. Even with imposing titles—which seem to lend legitimacy and authority to their roles—they are still thieves. They use intimidation or violence, and hoard what they have stolen. Bullies actually brag about these takings as evidence of their superiority, and make a show of their wealth, but they justify themselves only if needed to preserve their power and plunder. We should always call them by what they are: *bullies*.

- ***Parasites** take by stealth and deceit*. They *hide their stealing* with misdirection and lies, dressed up in social, business, political, charitable or religious disguises. They may work with bullies to share in their predations, and if it is to their benefit, they'll assist in preserving the bullies' power and wealth. They are often apologists, publicists and propagandists for the bullies who then protect and feed them. We should always call them by what they are: *parasites*.

- ***Slaves** have their work, health, hopes, futures and lives taken by bullies and parasites*. These are not just those in literal chains, but all who are held captive by social, political and economic systems that ruthlessly underpay, undervalue and *exploit* them. The labor of such slaves *subsidizes* the bullies, who reap what they have not sown, and who credit themselves for the produce of the slaves. Virtually all the great monuments, buildings, roads, systems and institutions of history were built by slaves and credited to bullies. We should recognize what they have been forced to be, and use the right word: *slaves*.

To create mutual care, we must look and fully comprehend each of these in turn: the bullies, parasites and slaves—of history and in our present world. Only then will we be able, *together*, to evolve beyond them all.

Some of what follows in the chapters ahead will be familiar, and other details and revelations will be a surprise—as you will see. All of it is to make us wise in understanding the methods that keep us enslaved, and the means therefore to break free. That's the first half of this book: **The Problem**. Please engage with it fully before moving on.

Beyond seeing the chains, and working to release them, how do we practically build a civilization based on mutual care? What are the foundations, rules, methods, insights and practical skills to make it actually work? That's the second half of this book: **The Solution**. Please take it in comprehensively, and then *add to it yourself.* I'll provide the means to do that at **MutualCare.online**.

Mutual care is something we can only do together, so let's begin.

DISCARDING A MYTH

Some people argue that our violent human history is actually the outworking of evolution and natural selection, with the "apex predator" perched atop the less-successful predators and prey, each in its place in the ladder of power, the bullies above and their victims down below. This, they claim, is "survival of the fittest," being played out before our eyes and is the natural hierarchy we should acknowledge and accept.

The claim is utter nonsense.

In a lifeboat large enough for everyone, throwing others overboard and hoarding provisions does not prove your worthiness to be captain. It shows you should be in restraints.

Those who strive to ensure that care is provided beneficially to all, from the work of all, regardless of anything else—*these* people are more truly "fit" to survive than the predatory bullies.

The fittest ones are the neighbors who care for others just as they themselves desire to be cared for: in food, clothing, housing, healthcare, education and safety, and in the thriving community that results from that mutual care. Common needs outrank any imagined right to the diversion and hoarding of wealth.

Bullies may rise to power, but they are never safe. Sooner or later, a stronger or more ruthless bully comes along to challenge and replace them. That isn't strength, and it isn't lasting survival—it's a brutal cycle of domination and collapse.

Instead, we finally and fully realize that those who strive to ensure mutual care for all thereby ensure care for themselves and their descendants. This is what evolution should become: a cooperative future we build together. It is imperative that we do this, and we can. Charles Darwin himself hinted at this when he wrote:

> **If the misery of the poor be caused not by the laws of nature, but by our institutions, great is our sin.** (*Voyage of the Beagle, Chapter XXI*)

We must resolve to no longer let bullies lead our institutions or countries. We must stop submitting to, tolerating, honoring and celebrating them in history—and in our own society now, today. And we must not let ourselves be fooled again by their self-promotion, name-calling, threats, or the self-serving narrative of "apex predator" and evolution.

Even Darwin saw this. They are not the pinnacle of evolution.

Today, after countless millennia of bullies and their destructions, we finally can grasp that those who take cooperative action, who strive for mutual care, are the fittest. We must choose to be those who strive, and who nurture others to this goal.

We can do this by the *doing* of unbridled care for each other, and for our children: We will teach it by doing it.

Those who care for each other will create the future. It is the most intelligent way forward. It exceeds and surpasses the predator.

The imperative of mutual care will ensure human survival, with abundance and thriving for all. It is the wisest way forward. It is right. And it must begin with us.

PREPARING TO ACT

To begin, we must not see ourselves as the hopeless and inevitable victims of powerful people and forces beyond our control. We are not stuck and helpless. The more we know, and talk, and commit to protect each other, the more secure will be the future of those we love. Mutual care is our evolutionary next step forward—not just morally, but as a species. And we can and should choose it.

The chapters ahead will draw without apology from religion, humanism, history, science, economics, sociology, psychology, philosophy and personal experiences. They will expose, unpack and explain how bullies and parasites manipulate our lives—how they siphon our time, labor and resources to fuel their own power—and how we can dethrone them and replace their selfishness with mutual care.

They may try to scare us away from these revelations, to instill fear. Don't be frightened by their lies, sarcasm, derisive laughter or dire warnings. Those tactics are designed to preserve them, not to protect you.

And so: What follows will not be academic, nor journalistic, but *an intervention*, with hard questions from friends: you, me, and others who join us in our exposé and confrontation. It is meant to draw out your own experience and insight—by looking fearlessly at ourselves and the world we inhabit, its history and future. And then choosing together to change it.

SEEING THIEVES

Some thieves are obvious, others hidden, some resisted, and others tolerated or ignored. Some have become so commonplace that we have grown blind to their harm, and have learned to ignore, defend and even celebrate them and/or what they do.

The extent of this thievery is so vast, it defies comprehension. You'll see it here, and it may tempt us to abandon the effort. Looking at it, across history and into the present, will be exhausting. The early chapters will be dark and foreboding. But that is the vile reality they reveal.

Worse still, correcting it—globally, locally and economically—will seem increasingly impossible, even foolish, as we grasp its full extent and its grip upon us and our daily life.

But we must begin to put in place a culture that resists theft in its many forms and promotes our mutual care. Later chapters will reveal how we can, together, do just that: Light will dawn in the darkness—so press through. Comprehending the dark makes the work toward light more valuable, so it is where we begin.

The False Hope of Technology

False hope preserves darkness. In recent decades, technology has been widely promoted as the cure-all for human suffering—with promises to cure disease, end hunger, provide shelter, and entertain. And it *does* have potential. But technological advancement has also been used by bullies to hurt, conquer and steal. We shouldn't be so naïve as to imagine that innovation alone will cure this human evil.

We must not tolerate bullies and parasites, especially those who pretend to be our defenders. In the end, they always defend only themselves. We must reject them all, to gain freedom for all.

This is not a naïve ideal—it's a necessity. Without it, we remain enslaved and leave to our descendants a world of misery and death.

So let us begin to see how this thievery lives and thrives. We start with bullies, and will follow with parasites. We will then understand and illumine their captives, their slaves, including you and me.

BULLIES

Bullies take because they can. It is just that simple. These are the people who *steal* from others, and they are all around us. They use power, laws, police, bureaucracy, gangs, armies, weapons, intimidation, strength, murder, lies and propaganda to steal and hoard wealth and power. Their positions of power, whether in "government" or other systems (business, family, social) are used *openly* to steal.

Bullies don't hide what they do, or even bother to "justify" it—unless they must. Often, their theft isn't just out in the open—it's bragged about. Arrogance and swagger become their fame and trademark.

More, bullies regularly belittle their victims as lesser beings, fools and weaklings, and describe their own thievery as heroic victory over the less able or "deserving." They flatter themselves as our superiors. They protect what they have stolen with disdain, insult, threat, violence and lies. They imagine themselves as apex predators and promote that myth. They never admit to error or failure, unless as part of a broader strategy of seduction and manipulation.

If we don't see through this yet, their self-promotion is working.

TOXIC MOLD THAT THREATENS

Real-world examples follow. Think of them as instances of toxic mold discovered in your home. We might hope that washing or painting over visible mold solves the problem—but that only addresses the most-obvious manifestation. The real threat is deeper.

To eliminate the poison, we must go beyond the surface and *remove walls*. We must learn how to find and identify the toxin in all its forms and hiding places, or it will continue to return and harm us, overtaking our home and poisoning our family.

As we begin to examine the toxic examples that follow, don't be dissuaded by their extent and persistence. They may well turn your stomach or invite denial and resignation, especially if you recognize this in someone you have followed, respected or supported—in politics, religion, media or social circles. Don't ignore the truth of *what they are*, even if it is a wrenching, painful realization. We must begin to see this evil everywhere it is, or it will continue to return and harm us and those we care about. *Press in!*

SEEING THEM WHERE THEY ARE

I'll begin simply with a series of personal experiences that have come back to mind as I've awakened to the broader threats and depravities in society and history. This is neither "woe is me" nor "look, I'm important." Throughout this book, I'll weave in relevant personal experiences involving real people and real places—things I personally witnessed.

What I have written in this book is not merely theory and abstraction from an ivory tower. It's personal. Why? So that my stories will awaken your own experiences and insights. You must claim them.

Then, as we look at current and historical examples around the world, we must consider how we together need to respond. I am a passionate believer in peace and reconciliation. But this does not mean we should surrender when bullies threaten, steal or harm. Nor should I appoint myself judge, jury and executioner. That's what bullies do.

More on this later. It is important.

The Schoolyard Bully

It is a classic figure in the popular imagination: the schoolyard bully who steals other children's lunch money. It takes many other forms as well, but the core reality is the same: One student, with willing allies, will mock, rob, threaten or hurt other students—because he *can*. Teachers and administrators may try to contain or correct it, but they're seldom able, and it often occurs out of sight. Because the bully succeeds, a pattern is set both for bully and victim. Both roles even begin to seem inevitable.

When I was 12 and small for my age, on the school playground during recess, an older boy with two larger "wingmen" worked his way through the students, dumping perfume on heads, one at a time. The three laughed at the victims, the crowd pointing and joining in the mockery.

No student tried to stop them or resist their attacks. Why? There were three of them—and as children, organized resistance didn't even occur to us. What little resistance there was consisted merely of students ducking away and trying to avoid them, if they could.

I was off to the side with friends, talking, and lost track of their movements. Suddenly I felt cold drops on my head. I knew instantly what it was. Without considering the consequences, I spun around and tackled the bully, took the bottle and emptied it on him. His two large friends backed away, and a circle of students quickly formed around us, shouting.

Teachers heard the commotion, came over, pulled us apart and dragged us to the principal's office. What had happened was quickly sorted out, and I was sent back to class. The attacker was punished, and nothing further came of the incident. No one beat me up (or shot me) after school, though that could have been the consequence in another place or time.

I don't cite this story to brag; I wasn't being brave. Maybe foolish. My reaction was not thought-through, and I could easily have been beaten by the wingmen. I recall the event to begin to expose the many forms and methods of bullies, and perhaps prompt some recollections of your own.

Are we able to see bullies for who they are? How they steal our peace, our safety, our money, our land, our homes, our time, our hopes, our health, our futures, our lives?

Begin just by recollecting events in your own life. The tactics of bullies are more widespread and consequential than we have realized, and yet now more vulnerable to our correction.

Think back. Where have you seen them?

Headlock of the Gods

When I was in my teens, our high school had three tall, strong bullies who roamed the halls together between classes. They quietly assaulted other students for their dark pleasure and to display dominance. The three would surround a victim, and one would put the victim in a headlock and forcefully grind his middle knuckle back and forth across the target's scalp. This was intensely painful, and when they were done they left the victim in tears, with no visible evidence of the assault; it was hidden by the hair. The bullies laughed and added daily to their list of casualties, with some students suffering multiple attacks.

We all feared that reporting this to the teachers or administrators would result in being caught and bloodied after school. Even the teachers were intimidated by these three, and they strode the campus like gods. Until…

The leader of the pack was in the same chemistry class as I was. Our teacher, Mr. P, was a short, stocky, somewhat rumpled older man—a good teacher but not physically imposing. During class one day the bully student was clucking, rolling his eyes, snorting and generally showing arrogant disdain for the teacher and class. He and his buddies did this regularly in all their classes. To my knowledge, no teacher or faculty ever said or did anything, other than try in vain to ignore it. Until…

Mr. P had enough. He ordered the kid into the empty hall. The bully got up from his desk, snorted, and swaggered out of the room into the hall. Mr. P followed. From my far corner desk, I could see what others could not: Mr. P pushed him slowly against the hallway wall, grabbed and lifted him off the ground. He said something under his breath while the bully's feet dangled, then lowered him down and sent him back to his seat. I don't know where the sudden strength came from, but it came when needed. I'm sure the administration would have disapproved, but it worked.

From that day forward, the bully sat quietly, and the hallway attacks ended. Many years later, I ran into an aged Mr. P in a local restaurant, recalled to him what I alone had witnessed, and thanked him for his action. He nodded, smiled slightly, and continued silently with his meal. Those who resist bullies come in many shapes and sizes.

War, Free Speech and Drugs

Resistance to bullies does not always end so well, especially when those bullies wield great power.

In college I had a weekly radio program and a regular newspaper column. The U.S. was in the midst of the Vietnam War, and I was a conservative voice in the local college press. I was defending the war as a legitimate though costly effort to stem the tide of communism, which seemed to be overcoming country after country. We were told that we were fighting the battle overseas "so we don't have to fight it on our own shores."

The Soviet Union and China, the largest proponents of communism, were infamous for suppressing any opposition or speech that didn't conform to their policies or vision. The United States, on the other hand, championed free speech, a free press and the "loyal opposition" in its media, elections and vision. This was enshrined in our *Declaration of Independence* and the *Constitution*. More on these revolutionary documents later.

For our foes, two foundational documents were Marx and Engels' *The Communist Manifesto* and Marx's *Das Kapital*. But in practice it was more the propaganda and conquests of Lenin, Stalin and Mao, whose leadership hoarded the power and privilege of their nations, and the "re-education," jailing or murder of any who opposed them. Much of this persists today.

To my mind, from my reading, education and confidence in our country's foundational values, this war was a clear battle between evil and good, between murderous bullies and freedom fighters, set on the stage of a small, divided country. The North was supplied and supported by communist regimes; the South was supplied and supported by the

U.S. and some allies. For us, this war ultimately included more than 500,000 U.S. soldiers, of whom some 58,000 were killed and many more wounded, and suffering even to this day.

The early '50s in the U.S. had been a time of intense anti-communist fervor. Movies showed how communist spy rings operated. Senator Joe McCarthy and the House Unamerican Activities Committee (HUAC) accused countless writers, actors, politicians and others of being communists. "Blacklists" of people so accused kept them from being able to work. Julius and Ethel Rosenberg were tried and executed for spying. It was a time of great fear of the Soviet Union, China and communism.

The books, movies, hearings and trials all starkly portrayed the enemy's lies and evils against our country's truths and noble ideals. By the 1960s this fervor had cooled somewhat, though the Cold War persisted: a battle of theories and ideals between "superpowers," with local battles here and there at the edges of distant borders. Vietnam was one of those battles, and we were in it to win it, to stop communism in its tracks.

I had read *Masters of Deceit: What the Communist Bosses Are Doing Now to Bring America to Its Knees* by J. Edgar Hoover, then head of the FBI, and *None Dare Call It Treason* by John Stormer. I was glad we had Hoover and his FBI (which he founded and developed) ferreting out the traitors among us and bringing them to justice.

My faith in our values and leaders was strong, and in public, and in my newspaper column and radio program, I defended our efforts in Vietnam as a clear battle between evil and good, lies and truth. And then…

I had been personally receiving a regular update letter from the U.S. State Department. I used the battle reports in it to bolster my defense of the war. One day, I added up the casualty reports for the prior year. I realized they were a fabrication—an intentional deceit. They purported that our forces had killed more than the entire population of North Vietnam.

We were being lied to by our own government.

It was a wrenching realization. Like my 12-year-old self, I didn't consider the consequences. I just tackled the bully. I began to publicly investigate and challenge the daily fictions we were being told, and I spoke out about the lives lost: our brave young men and women, drafted and sent, or jailed if they refused; innocent civilians shot, bombed or burned alive by napalm; even enemy soldiers—many fighting for what they believed was independence from foreign domination, also wounded and killed.

It was hell. And those fighting and dying for us were conned by patriotic slogans and the force of law. Some two million civilians died, along with over a million soldiers from both sides, and nearly 60,000 U.S. soldiers.

My childhood best friend, a helicopter crew chief in a recovery unit, has undergone numerous surgeries over the course of 50 years, all from his time in Vietnam. Countless other soldiers suffered hellish physical and psychological trauma for the rest of their lives. Many were treated despicably when they returned home, both ignored and insulted. This tragic reality is well-documented.

Were there bullies on the other side? Obviously. But the point remains: The ambition and power of bullies results in deprivation and death for other human beings, civilians usually the most, and military as well.

In the face of this horror, are we truly expected to accept the myth that an "apex predator" is the pinnacle of human evolution, as a bully would claim? I may be slow at times, but I'm not stupid enough to believe that anymore.

What followed my awakening to the government's lies may shed some light on bully behavior—and perhaps stir your own insight and action.

I wasn't a big deal. I was a physics student at a small college. My radio program and newspaper column reached a small audience. I was a tiny fish in a tiny pond. When I turned against the war and the lies, I joined other students and teachers who were also opposed. We organized "teach-ins" to expose and debate the issues facing the country, and to oppose the draft that was taking our youth off to war and jailing those who refused. We didn't use violence or disrupt classes. But we made our voices heard.

Among ourselves we joked that the FBI was probably tapping our phones and listening in on our meetings. The idea was absurdly funny to us. As it turned out, they were. One weekend, some college friends invited me to a party at their rented house. A dozen or so of us, mostly from the antiwar group, went. Wine, snacks, conversation—pretty tame stuff.

Unbeknownst to us, the FBI had an undercover agent. He befriended one of our pals, came to the same party, supposedly bought a small amount of marijuana from one of the students and left—and suddenly the house was raided by coordinated teams of local police, state police and the FBI.

All of us were shoved against the walls. An FBI agent put a .45 pistol to my temple and screamed, *"You move a muscle, and I will blow your ******* brains out!"* I didn't move a muscle. It was all loud, high-dudgeon drama, and surreal.

Then something more bizarre began. The agents started searching the house, yelling, *"Where's your cell leader?! Where's your cell leader?!"* We had no idea what they were talking about, but it later came out that J. Edgar Hoover, the head of the FBI, believed (or at least asserted) that any students who opposed the war must be local communists taking orders from Moscow, and that we were organized into "cells" with local leaders who were being directed to actively resist the war effort. They never found any evidence to support this claim—because there *was* none—but Hoover organized his agents to act based on it.

(Do opposing countries work to actively undermine each other? Of course. But bully leaders also claim that local opposition must be from foreign operatives, with spies or misinformation or—how could any *good citizen* disagree with the bully's policies?)

What had we actually done? We had organized protests and teach-ins, and we demonstrated the effects of napalm on human beings—with a scarecrow—as they are injured or burned to death by it, and I had exposed some lies from the State Department from its own public news releases!

Those are all protected under the First Amendment to the Constitution:

> **Congress shall make no law respecting an establishment of religion or prohibiting the free exercise thereof; or abridging the freedom of speech, or of the press; or the right of the people peaceably to assemble, and to petition the Government for a redress of grievances.**

Those in power didn't like that we disagreed with their war and their conduct—bullies never do—but they couldn't openly arrest us for writing about it, or talking about it, or assembling to educate others about it, or protesting it. There was no evidence that we were spies in a communist cell directed from Moscow, because we weren't.

They couldn't arrest us for exercising the right of free speech, press and assembly *guaranteed* in our Constitution. So instead, they charged all of us with "possession, sale and manufacture of narcotic drugs." Felonies. All of us. A lie, and an intentional slander. To discredit us and our opinions in everyone's mind, of course.

Our arrests and trials landed us on the front page of the local paper regularly for the next couple of years. Some faculty at our college wanted us expelled. Friends stopped talking to me. A member of my folk-music band quit on his parents' demand. One religious leader at the college turned on his heel and walked the other way upon seeing me walking toward him in the science building, and never spoke to me again. (In contrast, my local pastor, Lester Dacken, helped bail me out.)

Not one person at school, friend or foe, asked me if the charges were true. They weren't. They were an utter, intentional fabrication to defame and silence us. I was arguably one of the more visible of the antiwar students (the sole journalist and radio commentator), but all of us were charged and our lives were pushed into turmoil, along with a ton of legal expenses none of us could afford.

This was all put into sharp focus decades later when John Ehrlichman, a top aide to Nixon, admitted to using exactly the strategy Hoover had begun:

> The Nixon campaign in 1968, and the Nixon White House after that, had two enemies: the antiwar left and black people. … We knew we couldn't make it illegal to be either against the war or blacks, but by getting the public to associate the hippies with marijuana and blacks with heroin, and then criminalizing both heavily, we could disrupt those communities. We could arrest their leaders, raid their homes, break up their meetings, and vilify them night after night on the evening news. Did we know we were lying about the drugs? Of course we did. – *John Ehrlichman (1925–1999), quoted in "Legalize It All," by Dan Baum,* **Harper's**, *April 2016*

All this drama took place decades ago, and our cases were expunged when the state supreme court, ten years later, declared the law under which we were charged to be unconstitutional. I recall it here for two purposes:

First, to show how bullies in power, *even within a framework of constitutional protections and democracy*, can and will use lies, laws, and manipulation of the structures of government, to achieve their selfish ends and protect themselves from opposition and accountability.

We regularly accuse other countries of obvious corruption and dictatorial abuses, but we are not immune to them. "Weaponization" is a recent term for using laws and government agencies to attack those who disagree, but the methods are ancient. Bullies find ways to thrive and crush those who oppose them. This is one of those ways.

Second, to urge you to objectively examine your own life and history. Where have bullies, lies, and subtle abuses taken from some to benefit others? Where do the poor subsidize the powerful?

And then **speak up**! Testify to what you know and have seen. Silence only emboldens them.

And just to be achingly clear: I'm not favoring a culture of victimhood, where we bewail our misfortunes (and imagined hurts), and find ourselves paralyzed by our bad luck and circumstances. Let us not invent or dwell in victimhood; but do let us clearly identify and speak out against the real thievery and abuse in our families, our neighborhoods, our culture, our businesses and our governments.

Also let us recognize excellence and integrity when we see it protecting us: in law enforcement, our military, and especially in the modern FBI. Let us learn to *celebrate* and *encourage* those who serve with care and integrity but *resist* and *restrain* those who seek and take power and wealth to benefit themselves, and misuse legitimate law-enforcement agencies for selfish purposes. Stand up to them.

LOCAL BULLIES: PROTECTION RACKETS AND APPROVALS

Protection rackets are ubiquitous, in cities, towns and rural areas, though often invisible unless you own a business or work within an area with licensing requirements for building or operating. It comes in two primary forms: toughs who offer "protection," and corrupt officials who withhold approvals until bribed or benefitted. Some illustrations:

Bullies Who "Own" the Neighborhood

My father encountered a classic protection racket shortly after returning from World War II. He had opened a small life-insurance agency in a suburb of a major city, two small rooms in an old office building. His goal was selling affordable insurance for unforeseen tragedy.

Two men appeared ominously in his office one day and said, "Nice place you have here. It would be a shame if someone broke in and destroyed everything. Pay us each week, and that won't happen." This was a classic mob racket of that era—since then largely supplanted by local street gangs doing exactly the same thing—and neighborhood store owners either paid up or found a brick through the window, or were roughed up, or had their store burned down (in an escalating sequence). Most paid up; it was a kind of tax for the "privilege" of running a business in a mob-controlled area, and it didn't matter if you hadn't made enough that week to feed your family. You paid the mob crew first, or you got hurt.

There was no benefit from your payment, other than not being hurt—and this is classic bully behavior. The store owners subsidized the lifestyles of the bullies or regretted it: an adult version of the schoolyard bully stealing your lunch money.

My dad was naïve about this racket. And he was just back from years of fighting in a war for freedom against Nazi bullies. Without a second thought, he leapt up and shouted, "You get the hell out of my office! *Now!*" The thugs beat a hasty retreat. I don't think they'd encountered such fury or fearlessness from a potential victim, and nothing further ever came of their visit. I suspect they never reported the visit to their crew chief. (My mom was similarly fierce against injustice. I guess I have their DNA.)

Organized Crime and Mob Families

As a teenager, I worked in a retail clothing store frequented by mob leaders and their soldiers. I was just "the kid," they were nice to me, and I was mostly invisible. I learned a lot by listening and watching. I delivered clothing to one of the leaders' homes. I once got a ride home from work from a hit man, in his black, chrome-less car. I got an education:

Most of us live with a worldview that "we are a country of laws," and that our laws are a common moral foundation: to protect the innocent and punish the guilty, where good efforts and kind intentions are rewarded, and bad acts and evil intentions are punished. We might suppose that there are some who take advantage even within this structure, but we do not easily conclude that our values are not normative for the world.

What's less common is the comprehension of how insulated and oblivious this worldview of ours is, and how it consistently fails to overcome competing worldviews. There are worlds within the world, and their values are *very* different.

I chatted often with the mob members. Their self-image was this: *We're a family, we have a hierarchy of authority (boss, crew chiefs, soldiers), we protect our own, and we provide goods and services to the public. When we steal from big companies—say, hijacking a semi-trailer full of goods—their insurance covers it, so they aren't hurt, and it lets us sell those goods at a discount to our customers because they "fell off a truck."*

The driver was usually let go safely. The successful robbery was later celebrated and the soldiers who carried out the theft were thanked for their work with a hearty "good job!"

This sounds a bit like Robin Hood—steal from the rich to give to the poor—but the targets, the marks, are not just big companies. Many sources of income do steal from the "little guy" to enrich "the family." But at that time, notably, most mob families drew a line at the sale of drugs—seeing them as harmful to the community and intrinsically immoral. It was a rare moment of selective ethics in an otherwise predatory system.

The key to understanding the mob is this: They don't regard the government, its laws or law enforcement as moral authority. It's just a competing gang, on a par with competing mob families, but bigger and better-funded. If you're arrested and jailed, you're a prisoner of war. Survive it, and you return to your post with respect.

There is no soul-searching about having made bad choices in life and now wanting to straighten up and live right. You *are* living right. You are *loyal to your family* and you *work to provide and protect*. Jail time is simply a price you pay for your faithfulness.

In the eyes of the mob—in their world and worldview—the country's system of politicians and cops is a competitor, a foe, and often usefully corrupt. It is an enemy, not justice. When a mob member is "turned" by prosecutors and testifies against the family, he is not seen as having had a moral awakening but as a traitor, and his testimony against his former family members as a betrayal of all that is right and good.

Let that sink in. This isn't fiction.

This world and worldview is not just that of "the mob." In fact, in many ways the mob era has passed and been supplanted by local "street gangs" and international cartels, who are organized together into worldwide distribution networks, most especially *for* drugs—which the "government" gang has declared illegal but some people desire.

This sense of family, our tribe versus your tribe, us versus them, is exactly what we witness with countries, alliances, cartels, militias, terror groups, religious cults, gangs and school bullies. In this worldview, right and wrong do not come from a divine authority or universal moral ideal. They come from identity and loyalty to a bully (or bully ideal), enforced by palace guards and parasites, reinforced by propaganda, and deploying every means available to harden the dedication of the slaves to the "family" into which they have been born, or been conscripted or kidnapped or conned, or that they willingly joined. Loyalty is valued above all, and enforced.

Many politicians, at many levels, have just exactly this "mob boss" mentality. What is just, and moral, and seeks the common good… is simply of no account. Loyalty to the boss, the bully, is everything.

Again, slaves are those whose lives and work are used to subsidize the health, wealth and power of those above them, and they are also the ones sacrificed to preserve this structure. They are taught that "giving up" anyone above them is the most heinous betrayal and moral failure.

Really, do we see the lie in the core of this? In this lie, loyalty to *our family only* is the highest good: the mob, the gang, the militia, the religion, the country, the tribe, the team, the leader, the bully at the top. Not any independent good. Not God. Not "the rights of man." Not a philosophical moral ideal. Not "truth." Not "fairness." Loyalty to family. *Our* family.

At least, that's the bill of goods we've been sold. Loyalty to the family, the city, the country, the army, the faith, the party, the soccer team, with a sense of belonging to something bigger, and protection from its strength and story. And a *willingness to harm* those outside of our family: that is *defined* as moral and just. It is rewarded and honored.

And we accept it as normal and right. Until the awakening to this harsh and bitter reality: Your value as a person is measured only in your ability and willingness to protect the predators above you and subsidize their lifestyles by draining your own.

It's one thing to have a group organized for the good of all—assigning projects, areas and levels of supervision and distribution of tasks based on need and ability. It's how *mutual care* works. It is something else entirely to have a group that's organized for the enrichment and protection of those above through the effort and sacrifice of those below. That's how predatory theft works. We must be relentless in building the first—and rejecting the second. Yes to mutual care. No to predatory theft.

We'll return to how mutual care works. But first, we'll unveil more of how the thefts work…

Approval Rackets and Local Ordinances

Our country—like many others—is filled with officials at every level, from local homeowners' associations to building inspectors, records clerks, village boards, legislators, mayors, governors and even presidents, who endeavor to do their jobs well and honestly, to the best of their ability, even when imperfectly. They consistently try to understand and to do what is best for all, not to enrich themselves. Every one of these workers will come in for unfair attacks, allegations and name-calling from others who don't like them or their decisions. These honest officials deserve our unyielding respect, gratitude and support.

However…

There are also officials and supervisors, at every level, who take advantage of their positions to enrich themselves: by embezzling, taking bribes, giving contracts for kickbacks, or even simply to assert their self-importance, to patronizingly exercise control or to micromanage even the smallest actions of those "below" them. In some places there is just an individual doing this; in others it is built into the system. Supervisors, legislators, even mayors and governors can be in on the theft.

When you are subject to these bullies and parasites, you play along, you pay, or nothing gets done. Major cities are historically infamous for such organized patronage and graft, but it arises in all cities worldwide, even in rural villages. Where there is power, some will use it to personal advantage.

NATIONAL AND WORLDWIDE: BULLY OFFICIALS AND PARASITES

In the U.S., we look upon officials demanding bribes—at least in theory—as *corruption*, as *wrong*, and we have laws to protect us from such thievery. We tend to assume these standards apply everywhere—or at least that our own officials and corporations uphold them even when operating abroad.

Occasionally, high-profile investigations uncover bribes in such dealings—going either direction—and someone will be fined or go to jail. Such corruption happens far more often than is uncovered or prosecuted, and now and then we see large corporations or individuals brought to public shaming for bribing officials or others in foreign countries.

What we don't know, or may not comprehend, is how common bribery is throughout the world, because—reality check here—low-level officials in many parts of the world are paid slave wages, or none at all, to do their jobs. It keeps more wealth at the top of these systems, and it is understood and approved by bullies in power that low-level officials must extort their income from individuals and companies (both foreign and national), or not be able to feed and house their families. That is the reality there.

Bribery and extortion—the thievery of bullies and parasites—are built into the system. They are how workers get paid at every level. In some nations, even soldiers—members of their country's official army—will stop vehicles and demand payment just to let them pass. They do this to feed their families. This is true. I've experienced this firsthand.

Officials further up the chain of command are well-rewarded by their government and by bribes from company executives or foreign officials. The slaves at the bottom live by scavenging from people on the roads, or from bribes for permits and approvals. (It should not go unnoticed here how this parallels our U.S. wage system for restaurant staff, who are paid far below minimum wage, and are thus forced to rely on tips to survive.)

Paying a "Toll" or "Tariff" for the Privilege of Movement

Tolls have ancient roots. Our turnpikes today, where fees are charged to drive on certain roads to pay for them, originated with thugs blocking roads with a long pole, a "pike," and extorting or robbing victims who were traveling. They would *turn* the *pike* after the payment was made. (The word "thug" has similar roots.) Cities and then nations adopted the technique to extract money and goods from travelers. Only in recent years has it become a method of financing the road itself. On a national scale, it is how countries exercise control over goods and services originating outside of their borders, either by outright bans, or "tariffs." This toll tax then is a source of income for the government. See Philip W. Magness' *The Problem of the Tariff in American Economic History, 1787–1934* for insightful background.

American corporate officials know if you don't pay up in one of these countries, nothing gets done. Bribes, at every level of government and business, are the grease that makes the wheels turn. No grease, no movement.

That's the truth, but it isn't the whole truth.

Bribes flow in both directions—though when directed at our executives and officials, they're often camouflaged: luxury hotels, fine meals, private transportation, attentive servants, lavish entertainment, expensive gifts, even intimate favors. All well beyond mere hospitality. Occasionally a government official or CEO is caught taking a bribe from a foreign entity. Public outrage follows. Maybe a fine, maybe jail for one or two people. What we miss is this: only the most inept bribe-taking—cash or bank transfers—gets caught, because a sloppy trail is left behind. And only a scapegoat or two are punished. Executive leadership usually walks free, though the company and its shareholders may pay a fine. The system stays intact. Everyone carries on, a bit more cautious.

So why aren't we rigorous in pursuing such corruption? Because in many of the countries where this is the norm of the entire political and corporate structure, labor is cheap. Cheap because the people at the bottom are economic slaves under rigorous oppressive systemic control, enriching the bullies above them, and providing us with cheap goods. It's not only their local bullies and parasites they're subsidizing—they're subsidizing us. Our lives are made easier, more affordable by their slave labor. We become the parasites, draining their lifeblood for our comfort.

You may want to quit here and read something easier. But if you do, you'll miss the uncomfortable truth—and the chance to do something about it.

This reality check is painful. It's agonizing even to write, but it's our world. It is the *opposite* of mutual care. Heaven help us if we think this illustrates the apex of human evolution, or the fulfillment of any religious faith or social ideal.

Our political and corporate leaders *can* change this, but they won't unless we insist. And if that brings economic discomfort—higher prices—then we'll likely stop insisting and look away. Unless we choose the moral good, the righteous path, and begin to care for others just as we wish to be cared for. Otherwise, slavery for our benefit will continue. This caring isn't about being a "do-gooder" or a "bleeding heart." It's the wisdom to see that we all have more abundance when the stealing and hoarding by bullies and parasites is stopped. Make no mistake: This rarely advances with self-righteous posturing. It advances through steady and relentless insistence on exposing bullies and constantly defending and lifting the most abused and exploited from their social slavery.

BULLIES IN HISTORY

How did we get here?

Alexander the Great (356–322 B.C.E.) became king of Macedonia (roughly modern-day Greece and Bulgaria) at age 20. His empire would ultimately stretch from the Atlantic Ocean and around the Mediterranean Sea into Northern Africa and India. In its wake, Greek gods and culture were imposed on the many and diverse peoples he conquered. This brutal legacy shaped our modern world in ways we often don't realize. The effects of his efforts reach and affect every continent.

He led the slaughter of hundreds of thousands, and his armies overran virtually the entire Western world. His battle tactics and leadership are studied in military training schools to this day.

Alexander studied under Aristotle, who was taught by Plato, who was taught by Socrates. These three are universally known as the fathers of Greek philosophy. Every educated person, in every country in the world, knows their names. They were geniuses whose ideas changed the world. Their teachings form the foundation of much modern political, social and ethical thought. Alongside them, other Greek thinkers—like Eratosthenes and Pythagoras—shaped the development of mathematics and science across the world. Yet they were also products of their own brutal history and culture, and those values still echo in their influence.

Alexander and his successors "Hellenized" his empire by imposing the Greek language, religion and culture on every nation and people he conquered. Local leaders and armies were killed, and the remaining leaders and people were brought under Greek leadership, teaching and control. This was not a trivial thing, and at times, even practicing a religion other than the imposed Greek religion (many gods in the heavens, and top human leaders regarded as gods in the flesh) was punishable by death.[1]

In fact, this is why the Christian New Testament was written in Greek, not Hebrew or Aramaic. It was the daily language across the empire.

Even the Hebrew ("Old") Testament was translated into Greek by the Jewish leadership into what is called the *Septuagint* (circa 200 B.C.E.), specifically because Hebrew was no longer a common part of Jewish daily experience, and they wanted their people to be able to hear and understand their own history and values in a language they understood—Greek.

Alexander was a bully. His conquests killed hundreds of thousands and established a legacy of systemic slavery that lasted centuries. Slavery was not just tolerated—it was *law*. It was the philosophical backdrop of the very thinkers we still revere today, who themselves owned slaves. Because of his conquests, ancient Greek worldviews and methods persist in religion and modern thought today in obvious ways (mathematics, philosophy, rhetoric, apologetics), but also hidden in plain sight. Maimonides and Thomas Aquinas, hugely influential in Jewish and Christian theology, directly incorporated Aristotle in their writings. Jewish, Christian and Islamic theologies inherited Greek dialectic traditions. We still think, speak and argue using these frameworks. Even our form of government descends largely from Greek and Roman democratic models.

We are largely oblivious to this ubiquitous influence, but it lives on in the very way we are trained to think and talk. Modern logic and rhetoric are based on Aristotle and the Greek philosophers. This legacy includes both brilliance and poison. Alongside philosophy and government, we inherited the celebration of bullies and the normalization of slavery. These have not disappeared. They persist in modern life—and must be named and rooted out.

Roman Slaves and Empire

The Roman *Republic* formed in Italy around 500 B.C.E., paralleling key elements of neighboring Greece's education and governance—including a Senate of wealthy, powerful men. It continued until 27 B.C.E., when the Roman *Empire* began. The Empire replaced the Republic after Octavian fought and defeated his rivals Marc Antony and Cleopatra, and Octavian

---

[1] See, for example, Josephus, *Antiquities of the Jews* (XII.5.4).

became the god-like all-powerful Caesar Augustus ("great king," with implications of divinity), with multiple layers of hierarchical top-down authority all the way to administrators in small towns.[2]

Many soldiers and innocent civilians died to make Octavian all-powerful. We see a familiar pattern: bullies and victims. What followed was the *Pax Romana*—years of Roman peace. Well, years without large wars, anyway. The powerful bullies maintained their power, slaves were owned and used, parasites benefited unfairly from the work of others, and the law punished severely any who disobeyed. Crucifixion was commonly used to display executed criminals on roads into major cities—brutal public warnings of who held power. Others who broke the law were simply turned into slaves.

Clearly, much of the legacy of Greek and Roman democracy, philosophy, mathematics and culture is of great value. But embedded in that legacy are dangerous assumptions—about powerful rulers, hierarchy, "law," slavery, and the ownership of some people by others—that continue to infect how we view the world. It persists, and we must expose and remove it.

For now, keep *bullies, parasites and slaves* in mind as you continue to review these bits of world history. They are a key to understanding our own world, and changing it.

Genghis Khan – An Even "Greater" Alexander

Genghis Khan[3] (1162–1227 C.E.) was buried with 40 horses and 40 virgins as a sign of his "greatness." In his life he overran most of the known world, from Russia through the Middle East, across Mongolia and China, down to India and Southeast Asia, creating the largest empire in history.

His cruelty preceded him. It often led vast territories and their leaders to surrender without a fight. Surrenders rarely spared his victims. He often ordered the massacre of every leader and able-bodied fighter, once even decreeing death for anyone taller than a chariot-wheel axle.

Those he spared—mostly women and children—were enslaved, robbed of what little they'd known of their culture, family and history. Here is a quote attributed to Genghis over his years of butchery and conquest:

> **The greatest happiness is to vanquish your enemies, to chase them before you, to rob them of their wealth, to see those dear to them bathed in tears, to clasp to your bosom their wives and daughters.**

---

[2] Notably, this administrative structure was adopted by the early church after the emperor Constantine (c. 272–337 C.E.) became a Christian, and it is reflected to this day in the hierarchical organization of the Roman Catholic Church.

[3] *Khan* is a title, meaning king or ruler.

Some bullies never go far beyond stealing lunch money. But others, as they watch their bullying tactics succeed again and again, finally cross a line, and move from threats and intimidation to outright murder.

When this killing first occurs, it may have been carefully planned and executed, or an unplanned response to being resisted in the act of robbery—or any of a thousand other causes. But the line is crossed, and taking a life becomes just another useful act in sustaining oneself in power.

The first death of a bully's heart comes when he chooses to take simply because he can, victimizing others for his benefit. A final heart-death occurs when he takes a life for power or wealth. Then one, or a thousand, or a million. Murder becomes mere arithmetic.

It is estimated that over Genghis' long life of conquest, he and his soldiers murdered some 70 million human beings, destroyed rural areas, villages and towns, cultures and traditions, and imposed his rulers throughout. The destruction was so vast that it literally changed the environment.

Some historians say he was "tolerant of other religions"—hardly praise for one who killed followers of all religions with equal cruelty. He said:

> **I am the flail of God. If you had not committed great sins, God would not have sent a punishment like me upon you.**

Many "great" bullies in history claim to be gods or the agents of God. Some of them actually believe it. Others simply use it as a tool to frighten and manipulate those they oppress. Whether delusion or propaganda, it works.

Finally, Genghis spoke the words that best characterize those who see themselves as apex predators, and others as threats to their success: *"It is not sufficient that I succeed—all others must fail."*

Some still celebrate and honor "The Great Genghis Khan." The millions of families he murdered and enslaved would not. We must not.

The imperative to refuse the celebration of bullies could not be more clear. They murder, steal, hoard and exalt themselves as the apex of evolution. Dead end, not apex, should be their epitaph.

We can choose to craft a world of mutual care, or we can continue to serve bullies who take pleasure in pain they impose. They will prevail if we do not resist and restrain them. We must begin to behave as guardians of each other, rather than slaves.

Ranavalona I of Madagascar

Most of us have at least heard the names of Alexander and Genghis, and we may be tempted to imagine that their murderous rampages and reigns were rare exceptions in time or place. But their methods were commonplace and frequent throughout history and across the planet, in empires and smaller countries, even in villages and families. Their methods persist today, though often cloaked with proclamations of national pride or patriotism or honor—regardless of country or ruler.

So let's look at one more bully, and her methods. It is a good example to illustrate the pervasiveness of the problem, because on the world stage, the country and its history are largely unknown to most of us—Madagascar, an island off the African coast, about the size of France or Texas. Ranavalona became queen in 1828 upon the death of her husband, and ruled as absolute monarch until her death in 1861.

As respectful and protective as we might wish to be about native or indigenous customs and beliefs, we must subject them to the same rigorous moral analysis that we apply to bullies and parasites anywhere. If they harm some for the benefit of others—if some are enslaved—if some are held by force or tradition to subsidize or protect those who impose rule upon them—we must judge it as wrong. No hand-waving or polite adjectives can make it right.

And so to Ranavalona. Her authority was believed to derive from a centuries-long line of rulers, divinely empowered by ancestral spirits and traditional gods, mediated through royal amulets and idols guarded by elite families. This tradition kept her in absolute power, and she elaborated complex liturgies and symbols of ancestor worship to ingrain in her subjects the conviction that she ruled by divine right.

When she came to power, she did not rule the entire island. So she forced her subjects into public labor or military service, then used her growing army to subjugate additional territories and impose her rule. Mass executions terrorized these regions into submission. Survivors—some one million—were enslaved, and their possessions seized for the queen.

These slaves grew to be two-thirds of the population of her capital city.

Deaths from the harsh public works, military campaigns, malaria during those campaigns, and cruel "justice" for any who did not conform, led to some 2.5 million deaths from a population of 5 million from just 1833 to 1839. Her "divine rule" killed half of her subjects!

Madagascar was contested by Britain and France, and both tried to influence or overthrow Ranavalona. They failed, and she isolated the country from foreign powers. She renounced a British treaty that had provided annual payments in exchange for abstaining from the slave trade. Though slavery had been outlawed in Britain, it had long been profitable for Madagascar—and Ranavalona fully restored its role in the international trade, as slavery was already normative under her rule.

She also banned all other religions, seeing them as treason against her authority. A few foreigners—kept for their specialized skills, such as making advanced weapons—were allowed to practice their religions, but any native who did so was put to death. Murdered. It is what bullies do to maintain their power and privilege. We should not celebrate their cunning in domination and death.

Bullies Today and Recently

History, even at its worst, feels much less moving when its events are distant from us. We don't feel the immediacy that we get from a war or terror that is recent, current, nearby. Time dulls the pain of others, shielding us from grief—but it does not absolve us of the obligation to see, to understand, to resist and restrain the bullies and parasites, and to craft a culture of mutual care. We must. Recent history gives us sharp exemplars, real-time illustrations, of dangerous methods and systems still at work.

The List of Awful Leaders Is Awfully Long

We've already looked closely at three notorious bullies, Alexander the Great, Genghis Khan and Queen Ranavalona. There were many, many more throughout history, and in recent centuries: Stalin, Hitler, Mussolini, Franco, Pol Pot, Mao, Hussein, Assad, Amin, Mugabe, Kim, and dozens more—including countries ruled by a military *junta* but without a single bully at the top.

There are many awful leaders even today. We don't need to examine them all here to grasp the pattern. Frankly, studying them at length produces such disgust that we want to turn away. But we cannot afford to. A more extended list is at *Bullies in History* at **BPS.online**. It can lead us on, as needed. For now, let it sink in—for our shared future—just how cruel, ruthless and self-serving such "leaders" have been *and still are*.

Bullies care about themselves only. They would torture you and those you love without a second thought, for their own preservation and pleasure. That is not exaggeration. They live and thrive by consuming lives by the thousands and millions. They are the deadliest of all plagues.

Such evil ones must never be seen as the apex of evolution. The only peaks they sit upon are piles of stolen wealth, stacked atop the bodies of the slaves whose lives they exploited—and the bodies of those they murdered or ruled.

We must redefine the apex ourselves. Those most worthy of honor—whose stories should be told and lives imitated—are those who give themselves to the care of others, and to the teaching, modeling and doing of it. If there is to be a promised land, it will be one where life, health, food, shelter, education and safety are provided to all without exception—and through mutual care, not predation.

Sacrifice means giving up something of value. In ages past, sacrifice often involved killing—grain, animals, even children—to appease a deity or get a good crop. Let's leave that definition to history. *True sacrifice is giving up something of value—time, wealth, comfort—for someone else.* That's the foundation of mutual care. It is what good parents always do for their children. When we pour our love and lives into them, they grow and thrive. When we spurn or neglect them, they shrivel, suffer, even die. We *know* they *need* us. With our sacrifices they can grow, mature, know joy and love and thriving, and in turn learn to love and to sacrifice of themselves for the thriving of others. Then all can thrive. True sacrifice gives life. False sacrifice takes it.

Are there struggles and disappointments in this way of life? Of course. That's part of the sacrifice. But the result is to increase love, health and abundance for many, who return it to us and give it to others.

When we sacrifice of ourselves to enrich and grow the lives of others, we become the true parents of the future, and the future responds with flourishing. This is the fundamental character of mutual care, and a universal truth.

Bullies sacrifice the lives of others to preserve their own, and the reality is, many bullies remain in power throughout the world. Each of them is or was celebrated for their cunning, military prowess or political ruthlessness. But they all fail the most basic test of life: to value others, and to build a culture where all can thrive.

Mutual care preserves and protects far more—and far better—than the exploitation of many for the sake of a few. This is not hard to comprehend. Now we must begin to live it.

Bullies will sneer. Let them. Their time must end—and ours must begin.

CHICKEN THIEVES AND NOBLES

Our culture, our education, our upbringing all affect and even determine how we see and understand the world and our circumstances in it. These can aid us in our seeing, or they can blind us.

Labels and concepts often impair clear thinking, and we will examine these more fully later, but consider this preview for the moment: A dear friend of mine is descended from Russian aristocracy; he's related to the Tsars and all the nobles of their era (1547–1917). Their reign ended with the Bolshevik Revolution.

My friend would often remind us of his noble ancestors, but when we would joke with him about this, he would say, "All it actually means is they were better chicken thieves."

His "modesty" about his nobility actually contains a great insight: Not only do we tolerate those who gain wealth and power by theft and murder, we permit them to claim titles that disguise what they, or their ancestors, have done. How exactly are such people "noble"? Yet that is the general term we use to refer to kings and households of thieves.

We allow their descendants to continue to retain the wealth and property that was taken from others. We idolize them and their celebrity, and gossip about their lives. They call themselves "high-born" and call us "commoners." We bow or even kneel in their presence. We see them dressed in expensive jewelry, walking through giant doors as soldiers snap to attention and as heavily armed guards protect their every movement.

Do important (in the best sense) people need protection? Sadly, yes, because there are bullies who would harm them. But we must nevertheless acknowledge that we ourselves allow theft and murder to be *honored by our language* and *protected by our laws*. Just consider the vast swaths of property, and the untold wealth, inherited by the descendants of tyrants—from mass murderers. Even their bloodlines are meticulously recorded, and descendants are rewarded from the thefts and murders of bully ancestors, and continue to benefit from them in many of today's elite institutions and entrenched inequalities.

What should we do with wealth inherited from thieves and murderers? Their descendants aren't guilty of their crimes, and may be very decent people, and truly some of them have worked for charities, justice, or sought reform from within—but do they deserve the stolen wealth? What about the descendants of those who were stolen from?

It's a serious issue. We can't just seize and redistribute estates or hand out random reparations to descendants of ancestors who were wronged, but we can stop honoring titles and legacies built on theft and murder, and make serious efforts to correct structural inequity created by theft.

Chicken thieves steal the chickens of others. That does not make them noble nor deserving of our flattery.

JUDGING HISTORY

Some might object that I'm picking on the Greek, Chinese, Russian or Madagascan people with these examples, so let's be clear: These are a tiny *sampling* to illustrate a phenomenon that is both local and *worldwide* and has persisted throughout history. These infamous names and battles are *celebrated* when they should be *mourned*.

Further, I would insist that our study of history is lazy and non-judgmental, wrongly passive. We tend to call mass murderers "astute" and "successful" conquerors on the stage of history; the territories stolen and destroyed become just a map and battle study of strategies and empires; and we count the *millions murdered* as mere statistics.

We think of all this horror like a giant chess board, or an online game of empire and conquest. Worse, it is often a morbid fascination, as if serial killers, school shooters, terrorists and tyrants earn fame, status, attention and even "grudging respect" as their killings are revealed.

We desperately miss the point with the bullies of history and today: Their victims are *real* people. They are *my* family—and *yours*. Our brothers, sisters, parents, children. They are all *our* ancestors. They are *our family* now. *Our descendants* will suffer as well if we do not change our world. This should make us disgusted and *angry*, not passive! What bullies do is wrong. We must be focused on the evil of their actions, not distracted spectators. We must judge history or suffer as it is repeated.

Changing this ongoing horror will be difficult—but it's possible. Just because we cannot instantly change the world does not relieve us of the obligation. All of the genuine progress of civilization took time, dedication, vision and a willingness to recognize what was wrong and work relentlessly to change it. Consider…

Working Against Slavery

Like most countries, cultures and religions over most of time, Britain has a history of conquest and enslavement and profited handsomely from the buying and selling of human beings, largely from Africa. The caste system and the slave trade were both the accepted, unremarkable norm of British life and empire. Many, in fact, regarded them as *necessary* to Britain's economic success and well-being.

A handful of British citizens, the Society for the Abolition of the Slave Trade, saw the evil of the slave trade and campaigned for decades to outlaw it. One member, William Wilberforce, a member of Parliament, in 1791 introduced a bill to stop it. It was defeated 2 to 1.

Their agitation and advocacy persisted loudly and relentlessly. They drew new supporters year after year to their vision, and in 1807, Britain at last outlawed the selling of people by people. It took another 26 years to outlaw slavery itself, in 1833, just three days before Wilberforce's death at 73. Some fifty years of hard work by many hearts and hands finally resulted in a change to immoral laws in Britain and its empire.

The practice of slavery continued in the United States and elsewhere, but this hard work in Britain finally led to its rejection here (and our Civil War), though its social and economic effects persist to this day.

The British law banning the slave trade prompted a treaty with Madagascar halting its participation—a treaty later *annulled* by Queen Ranavalona, a bully move. She banned religion among her people purely because the missionaries—who had begun educating even the poorest—were teaching that all people were equal in the eyes of God.

Such teaching threatened her divinity, her rule, and her enslavement of her people. Her forced return to ancestor worship—along with the murder of dissenters—was for the preservation not of indigenous culture, but of her power and position. Kings and queens tend to do that.

Her action was not uncommon. Other native leaders in Africa benefited from the selling of their own subjects and justified it. In 1807, the King of Bonny (now part of Nigeria) rejected British attempts to end slave sales, saying, "We think this trade must go on. That is the verdict of our oracle and the priests. They say that your country, however great, can never stop a trade ordained by God himself."[4]

Like Ranavalona and most bullies over most of history, divinity is invoked to justify thefts and murders. They lie when they say they have God on their side. They are not the incarnation of divinity but of depravity.

---

[4] Hugh Thomas, *The Slave Trade: The Story of the Atlantic Slave Trade: 1440–1870*, 783.

Resisting Evil When We See It

Wherever bullies and parasites exist, there are slaves—just as wherever there are slaves, bullies and parasites thrive. All three must be left to history. This happens only when our key motive and action is *mutual care* and the celebrating of conquerors and predators is refused.

At a minimum, every law we have or propose should be judged by this standard: *Does it promote mutual care?* If so, support or enact it. If it favors or enriches bullies or parasites, reject or repeal it.

To be clear, I'm not advocating universal passive resistance, or "non-violence," though they appeal to me at some deep level, and were used by Gandhi, Martin Luther King and others to great effect. Still, protecting others is a key component of mutual care, and bullies must be fought in manifold ways to be overcome. A robber breaking into my home and intent on harming my family would be resisted with physical violence; a financial parasite attempting to steal our home, identities or bank accounts would be met with detection, arrest and punishment. Those are legitimate methods of resistance to achieve our mutual care.

And of course, bullies and parasites will use these same methods (violence, arrest, punishment) under the *guise* of caring for us, to hide their true motives and actions, and protect *themselves*. The difference *can be discerned*, and *learning how* is one of the purposes of this book. Their evil must be ruthlessly exposed so it can be seen. We must not condone ideological camouflage that hides evil under claims of "freedom," "faith," or "security." Evil is evil even when dressed in patriotic colors or the robes of faith.

We can *resist* evil when we can *see it*, and we *must*.

BULLIES: IN CONCLUSION

Bullies often leave benefits—advances in technology, for instance—in the course of their aggression. Weapons technology, created for war, often advances technology in normal civilian life. But repurposing what evil created is not the same as endorsing evil to serve our comfort.

Bullies thrive under the cover of allegiance. We must see and oppose all these techniques of bullies, *especially* when used by those on our "side" of any issue: social, political, religious, philosophical, and so on. It is easy to see and oppose evil action when a foe employs it, but if we permit it anywhere in the fabric of our own society, it will turn on us. "Our" bullies only favor us for as long as it benefits them. We are dispensable to them. Not friends. Not family. Allies only while needed. Pawns.

In chess and in the real world, kings never sacrifice themselves to save others. They sacrifice others to save themselves.

PARASITES

Parasites take by stealth and deceit. They hide what they *steal*. While true bullies often steal right out in the open, because they can, parasites are those thieves who steal secretly, by stealth, lies, deception and misdirection. Some of this is independent of the thefts by the bullies, and some is in concert with them. Often they are the palace guards who surround bully leaders and polish their reputations.

Remora are small fish that stick themselves on sharks and feed off the scraps from the shark's victims. They're protected from predators by being attached to the shark, grooming its body and eating smaller parasites. This happens in our world too. We have human remora, who feed off the victims of bullies, stick close for protection and keep the bullies looking neat and clean.

Whether their stealing is in concert with bullies or independent of them, human parasites hide in the shadows, and conceal their own thievery rather than proudly display it as a bully might. They see their victims as "suckers" and "marks" not smart enough to know they've been robbed.

While bullies revel in celebrity, parasites tend to avoid it. Both use whatever means are needed to maintain their wealth and safety, including lying about what they are doing and why.

Plainly, thieves fall upon a spectrum from public to hidden, bully to parasite, and often embody traits from each, as needed. But what's true about both is: *They steal and hoard.*

It is often difficult to be clear-eyed about these issues because we live in a world filled with propaganda. The most ham-handed and obvious is easily seen, but the most effective and insidious isn't obvious at all, and it needs unveiling. We will wrestle with that in more depth in the upcoming chapter "Propaganda." It will prove valuable, I promise.

Right now, let's focus on human parasites, and how they work to drain us without our knowing, with methods like mosquitoes, tapeworms and ticks. Knowing how they dupe us helps keep us from falling prey to them.

The following parasitic techniques are among the most important to be able to recognize, in personal relationships, in social and religious groups, in business and politics—locally, nationally and internationally:

- Begging
- Skimming
- Misdirection
- Numbing
- Conspiracy
- Embezzlement
- Hiding
- Lying
- Distraction
- Entertainment
- Conning
- Evil Laws

These will often overlap and intertwine. Some illustrations below will help us to spot these, often hidden in plain sight, in our common life, culture, politics, religion, commerce and entertainment.

It is not hyperbole to say that human and systemic parasites abound in our lives—real thieves hiding in the real world. Exposing their disguises and reducing their success is a vital survival effort, for us and others whose lives are being drained by them.

So let's consider some illustrations of how human parasites work to beguile and rob us. We'll start with smaller and closer-to-home instances to sensitize us to their techniques, making them easier to spot in the wild (i.e. in government, business, politics, religions, institutions, media, culture). For more real-life examples, see ***Sources***.

BEGGING

Sadly, many individuals and families are destitute, beaten-down and living on the margins of society—under bridges, in shelters, on the street. Many of them have tried to escape their circumstances and, for reasons largely beyond their control or desire, have failed. They are stuck. Helping them up and out is absolutely right, and those who do deserve our gratitude. We all need to actively support any such efforts.

However, among the truly needy are begging parasites who prey on our sympathies, taking but never giving. They are dedicated to playing the victim, extracting care, comfort, money and more from churches, synagogues, temples, mosques, charities, government programs and kind-hearted individuals. When one well runs dry (or simply tires of them), they move on to the next one, with the same well-crafted story.

It's important not to assume that anyone begging is a parasite. In fact, in my experience, *most* of those who beg, or who are on the street or in shelters, are truly victims—slaves to addictions, or mental disease, or made destitute by sorry circumstance and abuse. They surely need us, and we should do anything we can to help them.

But the ones begging with lies and invented victimizations are, bluntly, parasites. They must not be pitied or enabled. By their lies and begging, they *steal* and divert what should have gone to those in genuine need.

Resist and restrain them.

SKIMMING PENNIES, PAPER AND ACCOUNTS PAYABLE

Probably the most common form of stealing, aside from more visible thefts like shoplifting, burglary or auto theft, is *skimming*. This is where someone, usually an employee, takes a little bit of the goods or money of a business or household over time, but not enough to be noticed. The variety is endless—reams of paper, an unused laptop, a few packages or gallons of this or that from the stockroom.

In days past, when small stores didn't have cash registers or video monitors, clerks could shortchange customers, or steal a little bit of cash each day from the till. It still happens, if not as easily.

Larger and Larger

New methods allow far greater sums to be skimmed digitally, at a distance.

I know of one bank programmer whose job was to maintain the program that computed interest on customers' accounts. Because the calculation often included fractions of a cent, he diverted them all into his own account. No one noticed anything suspicious in any account statement—they were *accurate to the penny*—and over time millions of dollars accumulated in his skimming account. The mere size of his personal account drew auditors' attention, and he was caught.

Some try to excuse this and say, "No one really got hurt. These were just tiny amounts from many accounts." But it's *stealing*. We've uncovered versions of it in our own family's accounts and credit cards. It is an ever more common method of theft. Check your own accounts for those benign-sounding small charges, like $1.95 for *Tech Monthly* or some vague vendor name you don't recognize. It's just as much stealing as any shoplifting or burglary.

A Major Bank

What the programmer did by clever coding—stealing by skimming funds from customers without their awareness—was also done by a major bank. Using existing customers' identities without consent, the bank opened unauthorized accounts—checking, savings, credit cards, debit cards and bill-pay services. They forged signatures, created PINs, moved funds through "simulated funding," and even altered contact info to hide the activity. The bank used fake transactions to charge customers for products they never bought. They skimmed money from the customers without their knowledge. Details in *Sources*.

An Energy Company

Skimming by creating bonuses and stock-price increases with fake profits. The simplest version of this is to just lie about income, expenses and profit. This is common to Ponzi schemes, "golden circles" and some MLM (multi-level marketing) companies. More complex versions use accounting techniques and creation of subsidiaries to hide expenses and inflate profit. A major energy company and its accounting firm were caught doing this—to enrich the senior executives, of course—and both are now out of business and the leadership convicted. Details in *Sources*.

Supposed Charities

Skimming is also a regular technique of supposed charities. You've likely received calls and emails asking for help—for cancer patients, the police, veterans, children—but the funds raised go to the fund *raiser* and the "boiler room" of skilled voices and recordings tugging at your heart-strings and wallet. This is skimming, pure and simple, and it makes us wary of giving even to genuine, valuable charities.

Those in Charge

The skimmers are often those in key areas of responsibility or authority. At a company I founded decades ago, the accountants siphoned accounts-payable funds into their own accounts. The theft was discovered when the *skimmers* were *scammed*—by a get-rich-quick scheme involving fake diamond mines in South Africa. It was gratifying that they were caught, but our *money* was *long gone*.

Recently, a nearby city comptroller skimmed some $50 million over 40 years—funneling it into a horse-breeding farm, expensive homes and vehicles—caught only when a co-worker stumbled upon her secret account. Elsewhere, those assigned to help people in times of genuine need skim relief funds for personal gain. These are not true leaders.

To be clear: Skimmers are *parasites*, draining from your work and income to benefit their lifestyles, comforts and pleasure. It is *theft*.

MISDIRECTION – *LOOK AT THAT!*

My father and brother were both involved in stage magic, so I learned firsthand how many illusions and close-up tricks work. One key technique is "misdirection"—drawing the *focus* of the audience (whether one person or a thousand) away from one thing and toward another.

Both hands are shown empty, arms bare. The right hand flings outward, fingers dramatically stretched and rotating to prove it's empty. Your eyes stay locked on it—while the left hand slips to the waist, palms a coin from a vest pocket, and conceals it. The hands come together, rub briefly—and suddenly, a coin appears. You never saw the "steal" because your focus was expertly misdirected.

That's a simple example of making something "magically" appear or vanish. Professional magicians have very sophisticated versions of this. So do human *parasites*—only they *steal*, not entertain. And just as magicians redirect your eyes, so do some media and political narratives. They entertain or alarm while deeper theft or injustice unfolds.

Pickpockets

Pickpockets are masters of misdirection—taking valuables without the victim ever noticing. Often it's a team effort, following a practiced series of steps:

- *Identify the target.* On a busy street, one team member shouts, "My wallet's been stolen!" Instinctively, people touch their pockets—revealing where their wallets are.
- *Misdirect and distract the victim.* Another member bumps the target, apologizes, argues, or creates some small scene—just enough to divert attention while a third member lifts the wallet.
- *Hide the evidence.* The lifter quickly hands off the stolen item to an innocent-looking passerby. If accused, they appear shocked—because the evidence is already gone.

Like remora on sharks, these parasites distract while the predator feeds—grabbing scraps while your focus is elsewhere. Their role is to draw attention away, so the real theft goes unnoticed.

There are dozens of variations—some can do it solo—but the core remains: identify, *misdirect*, distract, steal, conceal, deny.

And this isn't merely about pickpockets. The point here is universal: *Misdirection is effective.* Many parasites operate this way. They begin with a loud proclamation of their own victimhood—drawing your sympathy and attention—while quietly robbing you blind.

You get robbed without knowing it, and when you discover the theft, your property—wallet, home, bank account, auto—is long gone, either hidden, transported away, sold or "converted" by legal documents to someone else's name. The thieves often hide in plain sight, offering sympathy, claiming similar victimhood, and winking knowingly at each other at your stupidity as their "mark."

Mark? What's a Mark?

This isn't just about wallets. It's a mindset. Parasites see you as a "mark"—a fool to be tricked, drained, and discarded. And they don't just operate on sidewalks. These everyday crimes are examples for a reason: they mirror larger, systemic parasitism. You're not robbed by accident. You're targeted—with planning and intent. So what's a mark?

A *mark* is the chosen victim of theft. Only amateurs grab and run or break into random places for things to steal. Professionals plan and execute strategies. They pick victims in advance, plot what to steal and how, and minimize risk of capture. They call the target their "mark" or "sucker" and see their theft as a battle of wits. They take pride in outsmarting victims. The adrenaline, the payoff, the damage—they enjoy it. This really is the mindset of professional thieves. It's the language they use in plotting and executing an attack or operation.

I emphasize this because most of us are naïve. We don't know how parasites see us. They study how to take what's ours—then gloat at our loss.

Pickpockets, train robbers, scammers, hackers, financial schemers, professional thieves and *tyrants*—they all operate by strategy. They steal to fund their comfort and congratulate themselves afterward. Parasites.

Reading about pickpockets may be entertaining, but the *eureka* moment comes when we realize the same tactics are used in our social structures, our caste system (yes, we have one), our corporations, our governments—and that this has persisted through history, and it persists worldwide today. You're its victim right now. You're enslaved by it right now.

It is an unhappy but necessary realization if we are ever to create mutual care and *help each other* thrive.

Misdirection works by shifting your attention away from what matters—in order to steal it from you. It works. Your best defense is to know how it works—and to keep your eyes on what is truly valuable.

EXTORTION

Extortion is the use of threats—of harm, scandal, or exposure—to force someone to hand over money or comply with demands. It may involve exposing *actual* wrongdoing—or fabricating accusations of it—such as sexual, emotional or physical abuse, crime, lies, and more. Both real and "made-up" bad acts are used to manipulate victims into paying money or making coerced decisions—often to control, humiliate or force compliance through the threat of exposure. Others, like whistleblowers, are threatened with firing if they do not keep quiet about the flaws they have found—recent plane disasters are a tragic example of just this.

Madness of Mobs

This same effect—of strong emotions of excitement, joy or fear—is used consciously *by parasites* in mass rallies and strident crusades—of nations and movements—to *numb your brain* into making *bad choices*. This *cultivated* madness empowers lynchings, inquisitions, the execution of heretics and the jailing and torture of political and religious opponents. It even energizes the bullying of the kid on the playground and the shunning of the nonconformist, but the pattern set there ramps up from small-scale to large-scale, into religious violence and state brutality.

Be wary of going along with the crowd. There's often a parasite at the helm.

Free Drinks and Hospitality

Another common version of "numbing" is the ready supply of free drinks to gamblers in casinos. Every game is already structured to favor the house—it's how those grand buildings (or tiny storefronts) get funded and prosper, but *numbing* customers' logic and judgment improves the odds even further. There's no such thing as a free drink when decisions are at stake. You pay for it in losses.

There's a related tactic in corporate, contract or diplomatic negotiations. You travel to another city or country, arrive jet-lagged or sleep-deprived, and your gracious hosts greet you with lavish meals, drinks and late-night hospitality. By the time you sit down to negotiate, your brain has been numbed, and your side concedes far more than it should. Because a parasite *steals* from you.

Later, these compromises may be characterized as necessary to reach a deal, but the hard truth is you have been *robbed*—slowly, politely and with a smile. Veteran negotiators know this ploy well and take steps to arrive early, rest, and decline the pre-meeting charm offensives.

Make no mistake: If you are faced with any kind of decision-making, a parasite on the other side of the table will try to impair your judgment—often disguised as hospitality and friendly glad-handing, or even excessive personal praise that floods your brain with chemicals and makes you unwary and compliant. *Numbing works*. Watch for it.

CONSPIRACY ISN'T ALL THEORY

Conspiracy has two main forms: first, where two or more people agree to commit an act together, and second, where a false reality is invented and used as a means to manipulate, deceive and steal from a person or group.

To Commit an Act Together

One kind of conspiracy can be for good purposes or ill. A surprise birthday party is a conspiracy, where we conspire to bring joy to someone we love. But conspiracy can also be a secretive plan to harm or rob another. In current United States law, both the crime itself and the plotting of the crime (the actual *conspiracy*) are illegal, and the plotting is punished in addition to the crime—or even simply on its own, even if the crime that was planned is never executed. There is also a special category of this, a plot against the government, *seditious conspiracy*.

More pertinently, conspiracies by those in power target the governed—or rival nations and groups. This kind of conspiracy has forms that objective observers would find most foul, but also has forms that are elevated by some advocates as being genius on the part of those in power. There is an entire genre of "Machiavellian" literature devoted to this; see *Training Bullies* at **Sources**.

Worse, these forms of conspiracy, by those who govern, are often not illegal but crafted into the legal system (laws and enforcers thereof). Our own country had "Jim Crow" laws that made it literally illegal for blacks to enter "whites-only" restaurants, bathrooms, business and parks, or drink from their "whites-only" water fountains.

If you did so, you were arrested, beaten, jailed or lynched. You were seen as a criminal, violating The Law and the natural order of society, and deserving of punishment.

In some countries it is literally *illegal* to criticize those in power. You are arrested, jailed or "disappear." People fleeing such countries, who have been beaten and had family members killed, then make a difficult and dangerous journey to another country to escape—and there are welcomed, cared for and given "asylum," or contemptuously declared to be *illegal* and *alien*, then *arrested* and *sent back*. How exactly does this differ *morally* from "whites only" laws and punishment? How would *we* want to be received if *we* had fled cruelty and oppression?

These, and a thousand examples beyond, demonstrate how bullies and parasites maintain or expand their power in government, and fool us into thinking it is good: *law* and *order*. I wish that were not so true.

We will deal with this issue more proactively in the second half of the book. For now, keep watch. Don't look away.

To Create a False Reality

The second form of conspiracy is the creation of a false reality as a means to deceive and steal from a person or group (right on up to a whole country or planet). This is done deliberately by some who are puppeteers, and others who are puppets who spread lies they sincerely believe. All to join their false reality and the assurances it offers. There are religious, cultural and political exemplars of this throughout history and in the recent past. And the creators, when accused, will often claim persecution and conspiracy against *them*. It is all fraught with deceit and distraction.

EMBEZZLEMENT AND CONVERSION

We often hear of government or corporate employees who are caught "embezzling" funds. This is a form of *skimming*, of course. But it can also be a large, complete theft, of a company, estate, or savings, by people in trusted positions who secretly divert assets for personal gain.

We had a very successful great-grandfather who—according to family legend—retired at 45, and would dress nattily and take the train into the city each day to manage his investments. In his nineties he developed dementia and was placed in a care facility. When he died, his assets had vanished. We suspect someone—perhaps a broker, caregiver, or who knows—found a way to quietly siphon off his wealth. This is sadly not an uncommon method for *parasites* amongst the elderly and disabled.

Hiding in Plain Sight

Parasites take by stealth, by being quiet, unobtrusive, secretive. This may mean hiding so as not to be seen at all, or hiding "in plain sight" with a disguise or camouflage that allows the thievery to go unnoticed.

This takes countless forms, including hidden transaction fees, disguised or misstated interest charges, "gotcha" charges or terms that may have been hidden in tiny print in a contract, inflated charges, renewal fees when no renewal was purchased, surcharges added to restaurant or other bills without the consent of the purchaser, and outright fraudulent and repeated charges that are small enough to often go unnoticed. These smaller amounts often cause minor irritation even when discovered, but others can loom large: $25 for an aspirin, or $700 for insulin, or $150,000 for a medical procedure that should be far less… and then "not covered" by insurance because preapproval had not been sought.

Nearly everyone encounters this kind of hidden theft in the course of financial transactions in everyday life, and we may fight them when we discover them, or not, but we need to now recognize them for what they are: *parasites*. *Stealing*, pure and simple.

Hiding is how they minimize discovery and dull our reaction even when we spot them, but these varieties of hiding do not minimize nor negate what is underway. A parasite is draining life-blood, stealing from you.

Grandpa, Princes and Rich Widows

Parasitic theft always involves lying. Deception is its core method. But there is also a whole subcategory of lying that is so blatant as to deserve attention by itself, and it usually targets the elderly or the young or naïve.

"Grandpa? I'm scared! I'm in London and my wallet was stolen. The hotel says they will have me arrested if I don't pay the bill right away, and my plane ticket and passport are gone. *Please* can you help me?"

"What can I do?"

"Can you send me $1500? I feel awful having to ask you, but I don't know what else to do. I can pay the hotel and get a really cheap standby ticket back home. I'm shaking!"

That was an actual call I received years ago. As I have no grandchildren, and know about these scams, I played along to see what the lie was intended to get—in this case, $1500. Not enough money to alert an unsuspecting grandparent, and a quivering voice designed to elicit immediate sympathy. This lie has worked thousands of times on grandparents, taking advantage of their commonly reduced hearing ability, possible declining cognitive ability, and even their embarrassment at not recognizing a grandchild's voice. Sophisticated versions do enough background checking to know the names of actual grandkids and where they may be traveling. There are endless variations.

With the advent of AI, scammers can perfectly mimic the actual voice of grandkids or other loved ones, pretending to be in danger and pleading for help. In other variations, the caller might insist he is a government agent, that criminal charges have been filed for overdue taxes, and only immediate payment will stop agents from coming to your home and arresting you *today*. The scammers are expert at sounding like law-enforcement officers and can be very intimidating and believable when they *lie*, to *steal* from you. It is what parasites do.

European Lottery

Quite a number of years ago, a 97-year-old friend was in a nursing home. One day while I visited her, she confided in a whisper, "I have a big surprise coming for the church." Much as I tried, she wouldn't reveal the surprise. It turned out she was being scammed. She'd received an official-looking letter from "The European Lottery," stating she'd been entered anonymously and won seven million dollars. When she called the overseas number listed, they congratulated her—then said, "for your safety," that she was sworn to secrecy until the payments were made. The money wouldn't be mailed, they said, but could be wired directly—"minus transaction fees and taxes," of course—straight to her account.

You can guess the rest. She gave them her bank info, and within hours her account had been emptied. The parasites had lied, as parasites do, and they stole the few remaining savings of an elderly woman. They doubtless celebrated "outsmarting" her.

This same kind of theft has countless variations. For a time, the most common was the "Nigerian prince" email, asking your help to transfer a huge sum of money from his country to yours. Or an elderly widow from Europe whose husband had been a successful oil executive, and now that she was old and dying of cancer, she wanted someone to have her fortune and use it for charity.

If it seems too good to be true, it is. Always talk to someone wise—friend, banker or police—before taking any action or letting any money go.

The Fraud Warning Is the Fraud

More recently, people are receiving emails that look like a bank, vendor or payment company is verifying you made a certain transaction—for software, clothing, whatever. Of course you won't recognize it and will think someone is using your card or another account to steal from you. It warns of possible fraud and urges you to act.

The message *is* the fraud. It may include a number to call or a link to click "if this wasn't you." Either option connects you to the thief. The person on the other end will sound official and "verify" your details so the charges can be reversed. In reality, they're draining your account.

More specific examples are in **Sources**. Never, never, **never** act on any such offer or warning without first checking with someone with real knowledge and experience. And never call the number or click the link.

DISTRACTION BY THREAT AND ENTERTAINMENT

Distraction is cousin to misdirection, but on a larger scale. It comes in two main forms. The first is the invention of an encompassing *"threat"*—something built up and reinforced until it consumes one's attention so much that the simple elements of reality, history, family and life circumstances are either denied, distorted or diminished.

It is an alternative reality that deceives and encloses. It's central to religious cults, political movements and groups obsessed with conspiracy—imagining dark forces beneath every institution: government, business, media, politics, even history. Dismissed by some as "conspiracy theories" and swallowed whole by others, these threats become all-consuming. Anyone who questions them is labeled naïve, brainwashed or corrupt.

Whether the threat is real, exaggerated or imagined, parasites exploit it. You're frightened—repeatedly—by a carefully crafted enemy, drawn into a false reality. Cults do this about family and friends. Politicians do this to demonize opponents. Governments do it to each other. They use scary labels, broad accusations and *dehumanization*—to blunt our empathy. ***They*** *are not family.* ***They*** *are enemy.* ***They*** *are not like us. They are* ***other****.*

The second form is *entertainment*. Something enjoyable distracts while theft—of work, money, power, rights—goes unnoticed or willingly surrendered. This is not new. Around 100 C.E., the Roman author Juvenal (*Satires*, Satire X) mocked his fellow citizens for accepting "bread and games"—free grain and flashy spectacles—in exchange for political complacency.

Welcome to the modern version. Like a shape-shifting monster, today's "bread and games" come in a thousand forms. Politicians promise benefits or to preserve existing privilege. The "news" becomes an electronic coliseum of shouting gladiators, subverting, attacking and maligning one another and their chosen enemies. The hosts and their owners grow rich. The bully politicians posture and grasp for power. Honest ones barely get heard or believed. And the citizens are distracted—entertained by the noise of it all. We live in first-century Rome. Only worse.

And here's the hardest part: Once you see this clearly, those still caught up in the modern coliseum's invented reality won't hear you. They've picked sides. Their team must win. The other must be destroyed. Refuse to choose, and you'll be mocked, shunned or seen as a traitor or fool.

It's easier to stay in the invented world. But doing so is surrender—to bullies and parasites. Your life remains enslaved, and your work continues to subsidize those above you. *The opposite of mutual care*.

CONNING THE MARKS

Beyond distraction lies manipulation—stealing trust to steal wealth. "Con man" is short for "confidence man": someone who gains a victim's trust, then uses it to access what isn't theirs. "Con" describes both the thief and the method itself. Cons *con* people—their *marks*.

As with other parasitic methods, conning can be simple or complex. Sometimes it's a flattering lie—the classic gold-digger or smooth-talking gigolo. Other times, it's as complex as a scheme in which the mark believes he's a co-conspirator in a get-rich scheme but is actually the victim. The con itself may be simple, like a job promised but never done: replacing a roof, painting a house, renting an apartment. Or hiring someone, then refusing to pay. Or short-changing an employee who quits or is let go. Or withholding *earned* wages or other compensation—commissions, royalties, paid leave, etc. The tactics vary, but the pattern is the same: promise, collect, vanish.

The con plays the odds. A few victims may sue or call the police—but most won't. The stolen down-payment or withheld wage becomes profit for the parasite. It's simple, common, and happens every day.

A more advanced con—the *co-conspirator seduction*—offers higher reward and lower risks. Here, the mark thinks they're in on a scam. The conman offers a supposedly fixed sports event, fake fine art, insider-trading info. The mark hands over valuables, expecting a dishonest payday. But when no money comes back, the mark can't go to the authorities, because reporting it would mean admitting to conspiracy to commit fraud. And if anyone *does* complain, the actual conman will deny the allegations or use phony records and paid witnesses to seem legitimate.

EVIL LAWS

There are times throughout history, and places in the world today, where people are subjected to laws, enforced by those in power, that can be easily seen as evil. These are addressed here under "parasites" rather than "bullies" because, while they benefit both, Evil Laws hide behind the guise of legitimacy—camouflaged as justice. The Law should protect you, but Evil Laws are used to take your liberty, property, time and well-being—without your consent and often without your awareness.

The more obvious Evil Laws include…

- government imposed without the consent of the governed
- prohibitions against criticizing the government, leaders, institutions or the laws themselves
- prosecution of those who criticize or object
- laws protecting monopolies or banning fair competition
- forced labor (in fields, mines, homes, estates or palaces)
- forced military service to enrich those in power
- discrimination by origin, genetics, religion or culture—i.e., racism
- discrimination based on disability (e.g., sub-minimum wages, forced guardianships or incarceration)
- imposed religious or cultural norms (dress, beliefs, relationships) and punishment for violations
- taxation without representation
- taxes levied in preferential ways to favor bullies and parasites
- punishments far exceeding the crime (e.g., cutting off a hand for stealing a piece of fruit)
- jail for victimless "crimes" (e.g., political or religious affiliations or associations, and some adult relationships)

But there are also less-obvious and even *more insidious* evil laws—those that facilitate the exercise of power and theft for both parasites and bullies, and that are often so much a part of the fabric of society and government as to be invisible to the unaided eye. We've learned to accept them, but it is time to refuse and repeal.

Examples abound—but exposing them often stirs a conditioned response. We've been taught to see certain evils as good, so when they're revealed as genuinely evil, we recoil—and default back to a conditioned approval or defense of them. After all, it's The Law. How could it be wrong? We have been trained. We accommodated. We got used to it.

It is how the bullies and parasites keep us in servitude. Their social narratives, their propaganda, have taught us to defend and approve of a system that holds them up, and us down, and we've been led to believe that this hierarchy is the key to success for our society, and for us. They keep us in our place. We accept trickle-down economics and even social-welfare programs like dogs hoping for scraps from the table.

Every law, existing or proposed, should be judged by a simple test: Does it foster mutual care, or does it unfairly benefit some at the expense of others? If it's theft, expose and reject it. If it advances mutual care, support and sustain it.

FEAR, LIES, LABELS AND NAME-CALLING

Bullies and parasites lie. We'll continue to pull back the curtain on their lies, but likely with growing trepidation, because we were trained to idolize our captivity and defend it. We will see this. We won't like seeing it, and may beat a hasty retreat from the specter of it. We may want to close the curtain and pretend the monster behind it isn't there. Or pretend it is our protector and the source of our well-being. I hope not.

The Failure of Ideals

When lofty social programs or ideals fail, it is often because bullies and parasites *use* these to draw support and power, then skim the funds flowing through them. They misdirect. They embezzle. They enrich friends and allies. They reward themselves with bonuses, kickbacks and high salaries, and thereby *steal* from the needy. They never intend that such programs succeed and actually change the existing social hierarchy to provide fair treatment for all. That would put them out of a job. They merely pretend to care and help. It is a strategy. They lie.

There is a glaringly obvious example of this, where the ideal and the evil have become so entangled that any analysis of the ideal seems doomed. But we have to start somewhere, so we must dare to look at...

"Communism"

Deconstructing communism—both the idea and its implementations—helps expose more of the lies that let bullies and parasites keep their subsidized lives of excess, and the fear, labels and name-calling they use to preserve their privilege. You'll likely find these at work in your own reactions as you read what follows.

The challenge to any analysis—and why we start with this difficult one—is that the word *communism* is overloaded with loathing and repulsion, especially in the West. This reputation was rightfully earned by evil leaders enslaving others and dressing up their oppression with idealistic slogans, "people's art" and military parades—while jailing or murdering *millions* who spoke out or resisted their oppression. Like other bullies throughout history, their reputations as "apex predators" proved not their evolutionary peak but their evil and cruelty.

So too the label and allegation of "communism." We *rightly* fear the murderous oppression of bully leaders and regimes that claim communism, socialism, Marx, Mao and others as their ideals and goal.

We *wrongly* accept the misuse of those labels to anything that aims to more equally distribute food, housing, medical care, education or safety. The wealthy already have all of those, and the poor do not. Those in the middle have some access, but a single medical crisis or economic downturn can quickly bankrupt any of us—and often has. You probably know someone. You might *be* that someone.

The mere suggestion that this cruel inequity is wrong and should be corrected is met with a practiced and damning response that equity is Marxism, communism, socialism or "entitlement," and that it will quickly turn our lives into the hell that murderous regimes elsewhere have created.

Are we capable of distinguishing the actions of bullies from the "ideals" they have co-opted to put and keep themselves in power?

Even *equity* gets twisted to sound like theft when it simply means fairness.

Redistribution of wealth is similarly alleged about equity and fairness, where average, middle-class citizens will supposedly have their income divided up and given to those who refuse to work.

These lies, labels and name-calling are meant to frighten us and stop us from even considering *mutual care*. They exist to keep bullies and parasites in power, preserve their *stolen* wealth, and *keep you in your place*. Thinking this through objectively, "*commune*-ism" is at its root an ancient and simple family and social ideal: Each of us contributes our resources and abilities for the benefit of all; in turn, each of us receives what we need to thrive. "From each according to ability, to each according to need."

Historically, sadly, this is **not** what became the operating principle of what is now *called* "communism." Instead, workers were forced to surrender individual rights, property and lives to The State. The entire workforce was flattened and enslaved, ruled by "glorious leaders" with ruthless control. ***That*** was *and is* the "communism" based on Marx, but used, of course, for the benefit of bullies and parasites. The form and the decoration changed. The reality did not: Bullies and parasites steal from slaves. The wealthy are subsidized by the poor.

Socialism—in theory—is a different economic form, where the people as a whole own major industries, but small businesses and farms may still be privately run.

There are many theories on how socialism can be structured, and various forms of it exist today in democracies around the world. In these systems, major decisions—especially those affecting public well-being—are made by elected officials and civil servants, not by corporations hoping to profit.

Healthcare is a clear example. Do we really believe fairness in healthcare makes someone a Marxist or socialist? Consider instead: If the care of an individual is based on profit rather than the person's well-being, the provider is incentivized to choose what *pays them* best—not what *heals you* best. That can never be a good thing.

Yet many of us have a gut-level revulsion when the term *socialized medicine* is hurled as an accusation, and taking a step back for a reasoned and rigorous analysis seems nearly impossible. We'll attempt that in a later chapter, ignoring the name-calling and unpacking the actual issues.

Our focus here is on the use of *fear*, *lies*, *labels* and *name-calling* more broadly—to recognize and not be manipulated by it—so let's consider some examples of communism and socialism in history and today.

We need to separate reality from mere propaganda.

In our public discourse, it is as if we have a bag labeled "bad things," into which we throw ideas and labels, thereby removing them from public understanding and actual dialogue. Do we know the actual histories of capitalism, socialism and communism, and how the proponents of each have railed against each other? In *Das Kapital*, Marx had laid the blame for all of society's ills on the use of *capital*—money—by those who had it, to control those who did not.

His theories fed 20th-century clashes: communists vs. capitalists, socialists vs. capitalists—and both against Western economies like France, Britain, and the U.S. Then Hitler, *a socialist*, turned on Stalin and the USSR. *Communists* fought *socialists*, and capitalists fought both. In the end, it wasn't about ideology. It was always about power.

The complicated, bitter histories and diatribes of each against each of the others makes it dizzying to grasp the real issues, especially in our public debates, and especially today, more than 100 years later. We find it easier just to lump together the ones that are unfamiliar to us and place them in a bag labeled *bad things*, where they can't really be seen or understood.

We will try in a later chapter to look at *each* of these with some careful objectivity. For now, some helpful though brief history:

Back in the USSR

The USSR—the Union of Soviet Socialist Republics (with *soviet* meaning councils of elected workers)—was a key example of communism being played out on the world stage. It began in 1917 with the overthrow of the Tsar, his family, and Russia's ruling elite.

This change was neither quick nor simple. Its roots are often traced to Bloody Sunday in January 1905, when thousands of workers marched peacefully in St. Petersburg to deliver a petition to Tsar Nicholas II. They asked for improved working conditions, shorter hours (10–12-hour days, six days a week were typical), limits on local officials' powers (who ruled by decree), and the establishment of a parliament—a minimalist democracy with a king.

The leader of this march was a Russian Orthodox priest, Georgy Gapon, a firm believer in the "Divine Right of Kings." Convinced the Tsar was a benevolent father figure, Gapon trusted that Nicholas would welcome this plea from his "children" to improve their miserable conditions.

Instead, the Tsar's Imperial Guard opened fire. Hundreds were killed, thousands more wounded, and some seven thousand arrested. The outrage that followed triggered widespread rebellions led by various political factions across the country. With the added chaos of Russia's disastrous involvement in World War I, the Tsar abdicated. He and his family were eventually murdered, and the Bolsheviks seized power. They promised power to the people, land ownership to those who worked it, collectively owned industries and businesses, and democratic councils at every level. Elections. Representation. Equality.

The *principles* seemed noble—shared resources, shared power—but the *implementation* was hijacked by the manipulations of bullies and parasites, who quickly entrenched themselves in control.

The new reality was chaotic and repressive. Workers were slaves of the state. Though local councils were elected and held some authority, fundamental aspects of life—food, housing, education, healthcare, safety—was still run by a top-down hierarchy. The label had changed to "commune-ism," but at the lowest levels of society, the experience was familiar: The poor worked; the powerful reaped the rewards.

Workers remained impoverished while rulers grew rich. It failed. The USSR—and later China—turned to expansion, seeking to absorb new lands, resources and labor to maintain their illusion of prosperity. It was a political Ponzi scheme: Steal from newly conquered populations to prop up those already exploited. It was propaganda masquerading as progress. It was a failure, a rebranded system of domination. The economic system was communism. But it was a system of bullies, parasites and slaves. Its long persistence in both China and the USSR came not from its success but from the cruel suppression of dissent— unneeded had it been true mutual care.

National Socialists in Germany

The same historical period that gave rise to Lenin, Stalin and the USSR also birthed a movement for *socialism* in Germany. ("Nazi" is a shortening of "National Socialist German Workers' Party.") Without recounting Hitler and his supporters' long, complicated rise to power, we can at least note that national *socialism's* advocates were rooted in bitter opposition to *capitalism*, which it viewed only through its worst excesses. Capitalists were cast as parasitic exploiters draining good people everywhere.

This demonization quickly took a sharper and more dangerous turn. Jews were imagined as the ultimate capitalists—secret rulers of global finance—and thus cast as parasitic vermin that had to be exterminated. Jews became the scapegoats. Economic pain creates an appetite for blame, and Nazi propaganda weaponized this into persecution of the scapegoat. Hence, the Holocaust. These ideas were laid out openly in the Nazi party's propaganda and academic literature.

The Nazi rise to power was so steeped in cruelty, delusion and propaganda that even after deep study, it still feels incomprehensible. I note it here for a specific insight: Germany and the USSR were, respectively, the proving grounds for the rise of *socialism* and *communism* in the 20th century. Their leaders denounced and belittled each other's economic systems with fierce public declarations and accusations, occasionally aligned when it suited their ambitions (e.g., the Molotov-Ribbentrop Pact), and ultimately collided in the deadly confrontation between Hitler and Stalin toward the end of World War II.

This clash, Hitler versus Stalin, was not a mere sideshow of the war but one of its central conflicts. In the U.S., we often have little comprehension of the length, intensity and propaganda-driven brutality of this ideological war between these two bully leaders and their empires. They both railed loudly and constantly against capitalists like the United States—and just as vigorously against each other.

Each system—capitalism, socialism, communism—claims the moral high ground while accusing the others of corruption and malice. Sadly, what begins as a contest of ideas all too often devolves into a raw battle for power. Bullies throughout history have always wrapped their ambitions in noble ideals to convince those they rule to follow their lead. It is the basis of nearly every conquest, genocide and war.

"For King and Country!" is the classic battle cry, used through history and across the world to inspire sacrifice and loyalty. But each bully who has invoked it has done so not for their people's safety but to consolidate personal power and wealth while pretending it's for the common good.

Every economic system—no matter its theory—has fallen victim to leaders who manipulate it for their own gain. We'll look more at this pattern and each of these economic systems in "Upholding Democracy."

For now, the takeaway is simple: Bullies will do anything they can get away with—without moral hesitation—while cloaking themselves in moral language to fool those they exploit. This is a hard truth of history and of the world today.

HONORABLE LEADERS

Have there been leaders who genuinely believed in and advanced mutual care, rather than personal power and wealth? Of course. Some inherited wealth or kingdoms but took that responsibility very seriously, living rare lives of caring and benevolence. They should be honored and supported. You'll find examples at **Sources**—leaders whose efforts toward care for others is real and worthy of thanks and praise.

But our focus here, and in what follows, is exposing…

LEADERS WHO LIE

The terrible truth is that throughout history, countless leaders have advanced themselves at the expense of those they ruled. They lied. They conned their followers into believing *their* success was *ours*—and demonized any who opposed them. They still do. They still want to keep us down and themselves above. We subsidize their lives. They reap the rewards of our work.

No more.

We *need* mutual care. It's the only path to real well-being—for us and the generations to come. It's not just another "-ism," but a foundational shift in what we value most and how we live—how we care for one another, our future and ourselves.

Don't be scared off by the proclamations of the powerful that what *we need and seek* is dangerous. They'll use scary labels. But the labels are lies. Their purpose is to keep you afraid—and to keep you down.

Because the real danger of mutual care is to *them*. To their stolen wealth and power. Of course they'll attack. Don't be conned again. Labels like *Marxism, communism, socialism, entitlement*—these are imbued with horror and ridicule to stop us from meeting our common needs.

It's time we just reject the tainted labels altogether—and affirm the one that clearly names what we truly want: *mutual care*.

"Marxist" governments didn't fail because equality was a bad idea. They failed because they replaced one bully with a new one. ***True mutual care hasn't been tried and failed***. *It has* ***failed to be tried***.

Recall the story of my arrest—false charges of narcotic sales, fabricated to silence dissent. That lie used every lever of power—laws, police, FBI, courts, public shaming. It was a coordinated move to preserve the power of bullies. A textbook tactic used across the globe and throughout history.

Bullies and parasites lie. Let's finally see it where we missed it before. Let's watch closely. Not distracted by some vast, unreachable conspiracy beyond our control—but focused on the lies right in front of us, every day. In the neighborhood. In the nation. Across the world. We *can* see them now.

> **When people learn no tools of judgment and merely follow their hopes, the seeds of political manipulation are sown. – Stephen Jay Gould**

Lies don't come with warning labels. They pose as truth. The method of successful lying is to make us think something is true, and to affect our behavior because we believe it or hope for it. Lies get us to act against our own best interests while convincing us our best interests and hopes are being served. That's the essence of propaganda—and that's why we need to learn to see it.

Propaganda is used to fool us. It works by presenting false accusations as truth, and by using noble-sounding causes to hide the opposite intention. It's not just about *attacks* on opponents—it's about feigning goodness to gain trust.

Bullies bully. Parasites steal in secret. Both take because they can and take what they want—using whatever means necessary to keep themselves in power.

Evil laws. Noble ideals. Enforcers. Threats. Promises. Fear. Distraction. Derision. Divinity. Misdirection.

They lie. They threaten. They imprison. They harm. They murder. They glorify themselves and pretend to be our benefactors.

*We—**only we**—can stop them. For us, and for those we love, we must.*

SLAVES

Slaves have their work, health, hopes, future and lives taken by bullies and parasites.

Slavery is the *exploitation* of some for the *benefit* of others. Slaves are not just those in literal chains, but *all who are held captive* by social and economic systems that ruthlessly underpay, undervalue and *exploit* them.

Our notions about slaves are woefully small and short-sighted. It is far more extensive than we imagine.

It is vital that we see and understand the thievery, predations, harm and murder of bullies and parasites, and we have begun to do just that. But it is equally necessary to understand their victims—the slaves.

Slaves are those whose work, health, hopes, future, days and lives are *taken* from them by bullies and parasites. The labor of such slaves *subsidizes* the wealthy and powerful, who reap what they have not sown, and who credit themselves for the produce of the oppressed.

Slaves are those trapped within a system that forces labor with little reward for them, to produce large rewards for others. The labels might be changed from "master and slave" to "employer and employee," but if some live high off of the poorly compensated labor of others, it is still slavery—the *exploitation* of some for the *benefit* of others.

UPPER CLASS

These others who benefit most are nearly always in the "upper" class, the most powerful and wealthy, and often see themselves as our "betters," an old-fashioned word for the condescension that often accompanies wealth or success.

This disdain is not true of all, of course. I've known kind, compassionate people who relentlessly dedicated their wealth and time to helping others and to healing the world.

And I've known others who lived largely for fame or conquest.

Even among the wealthy and powerful, there is a common "looking down" at *each other*. Those with inherited wealth are "high-born" and disparage the *nouveau riche*, the "commoners" who got wealthy with hard work, invention, good luck or theft. The newly rich speak of the *old suits* and *trust babies*. They compare fortunes and talk down about each other—and especially about the "middle class" and those below.

Middle Class

Here's an uncomfortable truth: If we are living in the "middle class," lodged in-between the wealthy and powerful above, and the "working poor" and poverty-stricken below, we are also captives in a system that *holds us in place* and *feeds upward*.

We subsidize those above us. We are subsidized by those below. We'll see this ever more plainly as we go—and we won't like it. We may have more freedom of movement than those further down the ladder, but that should not make us comfortable with a power structure that it is unjust to others: if not intentional, we are still structurally benefitted. Even if we're partly shielded from its harshest effects, a future controlled by bullies and parasites puts us all in chains.

Lower Classes

You inherit what your parents had. Yes, we all know the exceptions—those who rose through hard work, luck, timing, a great idea, and/or good circumstances ("the right place at the right time"). But they're famous because they're rare.

The norm, the unexceptional reality, is this: If your parents were wealthy, you likely inherited wealth and opportunity. If they were middle-class, you likely are too. If they were working poor or poverty-stricken, odds are that's where you remain. Systemic forces (education, policy, redlining, etc.) help maintain class stagnation. It's not economic gravity but enforced caste structure.

This must no longer be inevitable. It is profoundly unfair. And it harms *all* of us, as we will see in the pages ahead.

Slaves in History

When I began this research, I knew virtually nothing about slaves or slavery, apart from some biblical narratives, and that it was a sorry part of American, British and African history. I understood it as a tragic part of the past, with consequences still echoing nearly 200 years after Lincoln's 1863 *Emancipation Proclamation*. But that slavery, horrific as it was (and is), is only one chapter in a much-larger history—one far more ancient, vast and brutal than I had imagined. Cruelty, murder and enslavement spans millennia and the world. And it continues today.

If you have a moral center, you will hate what follows. Humanity's cruelty toward its own is rooted deep. And to see it clearly, we must explore examples from history—not to shock, but to build the vision and strength needed to fight it in our own time. It is far more universal, and *celebrated*, than we could imagine. American history is only the tip of the iceberg. The earlier examples of Alexander, Genghis and Ranavalona are only fragments of the vast expanse—*and defense*—of slavery. I won't try to reveal the history in full. Thousands of pages would still fall short. But you'll find extended sources and examples at **BPS.online**. What follows is meant to help us recognize slavery where it still exists—often hidden in plain sight—and brace ourselves to change it.

Your ancestors were *slaves*. That can be said with confidence. Throughout history and in all parts of the world, slavery was common, legal and "normal" in virtually every culture. Authors over centuries mention it in passing with no more outrage than they'd show for the weather. You have ancestors who were owned.

And you also have ancestors who owned or profited from slaves.

Some were *bullies*—those who victimized other human beings, stole their lives and work, bought and sold them like equipment. They had little regard for the care or living conditions of their slaves, often treating them worse than tools or livestock.

Others were *parasites*—those who profited from the system without owning slaves directly. They benefited from stolen labor, defended the bullies and shielded the system that fed them. Because they were enriched by the bullies' stealing, harm, murders and power, they turned a blind eye to the suffering of the slaves.

Bullies, parasites and slaves. Each of us have all of these in our past. Knowing our ancestors played all three roles—slave, bully, parasite—may, I hope, cultivate greater humility and solidarity, instead of shame.

WHAT COLOR ARE SLAVES?

In the West, our typical mental image is of "white" people owning "colored" people, because that was the recent pattern in our history. Slavery has never been confined to one race. The grim truth is that throughout history and even now, people have enslaved others of all colors—sometimes those who looked foreign or different, sometimes those who looked just like them. Slavery is not inherently racial—even if modern systems often are. Race is just a convenient excuse, rather than an actual cause.

Whatever color you are, whatever ethnic backgrounds you have, in previous generations your ancestors were both owned and owners. *Your* ancestors were bullies, and parasites, and slaves. As were mine.

We must *really* see this, as it persists to this day, and we've grown blind to it. We can stop it. But nothing will change with ignorance or denial. We *must* look. To broaden our perspective, we'll expose examples of slavery across history and the world—starting in the so-called "Western World."

Slavery Is Normal and Noted Only in Passing

Marcus Aurelius (121–180 C.E.), one of Rome's most respected emperors, wrote *Meditations*. Still studied today, it is required reading, especially in diplomacy and leadership training. Aurelius is widely respected as a gifted Stoic philosopher, and his insights into leadership and humility are highly regarded. The Stoics believe virtue leads to happiness, and the foundations of it are Courage, Temperance, Justice and Wisdom. Worthy ideals. Yet one of his most telling pieces of advice was: "Don't surround yourself with beautiful slaves."

Though he was counseling leaders against arrogance and ostentation, he reveals how normal slavery was. One group of people *owning* others was a common, *unremarkable* attitude throughout history. His advice reflected this assumed reality: Slavery is the natural order of things. He was hardly alone. Some 500 years earlier, Aristotle—Alexander's teacher—wrote of slaves:

> **Those who are as different [from others] as the soul from the body or man from beast—and they are in this state if their work is the use of the body, and if this is the best that can come from them—are slaves by nature. For them it is better to be ruled... (*Politics*, 1254b16–21)**

Aristotle here says some people *by nature* are only competent to be used for physical labor and therefore must be *ruled by us*. We regard them as beasts of burden, not equals. They look like us—roughly the same kind of body—but we are superior to them. They are *lesser creatures*, and it is right and proper for them to serve us, and for us to keep them in their roles. It is *the natural order* of things for them to be slaves and us to be masters. We are high-born. They are below us.

The slavery Aristotle defended had already been an essential part of the Greek life and economy for hundreds of years, in the mines, on the farms and in the homes. Virtually every "free man" owned at least two other human beings. Large landholders could own a thousand. When Aristotle died, he left 14 slaves in his will—just another line item of *property*.

Slavery in the Bible

There are numerous passages in the Bible that address slaves and slavery, though a fuller discussion must wait for another time. One especially telling example comes from one of the New Testament's shortest books, *Philemon*, which has been used **both** to defend and oppose slavery, and which offers a striking glimpse into life in the first century.

Paul's letter to *Philemon* (in Colossae, modern-day Turkey) concerns a runaway slave, Onesimus, who traveled 800 miles to find Paul and seek safety and freedom with him. Paul sends Onesimus back, but also offers to pay for anything Onesimus may have stolen or damaged. After all, as Philemon's "property," his escape was theft *of himself* and thus "wrong." Paul, seeking to free Onesimus from slavery and reconcile him to Philemon, offers to pay any cost or debt, and asks that Onesimus be received "no longer as a slave, but better than a slave, as a dear brother."

This was an extraordinary initiative, to be sure, but I cite it here to illustrate again how *unextraordinary* slavery was. Sadly, in our world today, it is still common—just under new labels and with new excuses.

Slaves Who Rebel Must Die. Spartacus Didn't Know His Place.

There were moments of resistance throughout history, but most slaves had no power to resist their overlords. They were expected to "know their place" and do as told—or face whipping, beating, starvation, or even death. Some were incentivized to obey: slightly better living conditions, a bit of independence, even promotion to oversee other slaves. These tactics are still in use today, just under different names.

Spartacus (103–71 B.C.E.) didn't know his place. He was a slave and a gladiator in the Roman Republic. Gladiators were arena combatants (think modern boxing, wrestling or mixed martial arts) who fought each other for crowds' entertainment. They often were to fight to the death. Wealthy promoters *owned* gladiators.

Unlike most slaves, Spartacus had weapons and knew how to use them. He chose to free himself, organizing a rebellion with 70 fellow gladiators that swelled to include 70,000 slaves and supporters.

Of course, this declaration of freedom was met with the state's power to crush the rebels. Slave ownership was *legal*, "*just*" and *normal*. These slaves were *breaking the law*, stealing "property" (themselves), disrupting the peaceful culture, threatening the social order. How dare they?

The Roman military crushed the revolt. Spartacus was killed in battle, and six thousand slaves—who didn't know their place—were publicly crucified as a warning to others.

Slaves, Gold and Genocide

One of the most horrific and revealing accounts of cruelty and slavery is in a lengthy account written by a Spanish friar, appealing to Spain's Prince Phillip to end the butchery and enslavement of the native peoples of "the Indies"—today's Haiti, Dominican Republic, Cuba, Peru, Florida and the many other islands and territories nearby. It ended in bitter irony.

Christopher Columbus had organized an expedition, funded by the Spanish Crown, hoping to find a sea route to India. India was prized for its spices and other goods, and the overland route from Europe was slow and costly. Columbus instead "discovered" the land and people of the Caribbean. Thinking he'd succeeded in reaching India, he called it the "West Indies."

Ownership of the "New World" was divided between Portugal and Spain by Pope Alexander VI in his 1493 decree *Inter Caetera*, later formalized in the Treaty of Tordesillas. The division drew an imaginary line from the Arctic to the Antarctic poles, granting Spain and Portugal dominion over all lands west and east of it, respectively. As the Pope declared: "Out of our own sole largess and certain knowledge and out of the fullness of our apostolic power, by the authority of Almighty God … we make, appoint, and depute you and your said heirs and successors lords of them with full and free power, authority, and jurisdiction of every kind." That is, the Church granted divine authority to colonize and exploit. Religious *justification* was deeply baked-in to the culture and world view of Europe, and the consequences of the exploitation persist there to our day.

This papal decree is why Spanish and Portuguese remain the dominant languages in nearly every country south of the United States. And with unrestricted power, granted by the Church, the conquests began.

They found *gold*. And what followed was a feeding frenzy of invasions by Spain and Portugal, the murder of *millions* of native inhabitants, and the enslavement of those who survived to work and die in the mines. The conquistadors—led by *hidalgos*, Spanish and Portuguese *nobles*—enforced their rule through soldiers. The gold mined by native slaves was shipped to Europe to enrich and adorn the wealthy and powerful.

The riches of the Indies had captured Europe's imagination. Nobles and commoners alike rushed to join the expeditions, lured by dreams of wealth. Bartolomé de las Casas joined one of the Spanish expeditions, hoping to make his own fortune. But once there, he had a religious conversion and became a Roman Catholic friar—essentially a working monk, dedicated to helping the poor and needy. What he saw so horrified him that he wrote a detailed account of the genocide and slavery, then returned to Spain to plead with the Crown to end it. Still believing in the divine right of kings, he saw the monarchy as the godly source of justice.

His *A Brief Account of the Destruction of the Indies* revealed unimaginable cruelties committed island by island, territory by territory, with specifics and numbers of deaths and atrocities. Here is just one excerpt of what he wrote, but illustrative of the entire content:

> **The Spaniards by their barbarous and execrable Actions have absolutely depopulated Ten [native] Kingdoms ... which now lie waste and desolate, and are absolutely ruined. ... We dare boldly affirm ... above Twelve Millions (computing Men, Women, and Children) have undeservedly perished. ... Now the ultimate end and scope that incited the Spaniards to endeavor the Extirpation and Desolation of this People, was Gold only... I speak of things which I was an Eye Witness of, without the least fallacy.**

De las Casas worked tirelessly for years to make the Spanish Crown, and all of Europe, aware of the cruelties and slavery inflicted on the local populations by the bullies and parasites of Spain and Portugal. Europe's horror was so great that the Crown ultimately forbade the practices—though they didn't actually stop. Spain then loudly claimed it had been *defamed*—a classic bully tactic: portraying itself as the victim.

Worse, in a bitter but unsurprising irony—because the genocide had so depopulated the territories, and enslaving the surviving locals was now technically illegal—the Crown approved a new practice: *importing new slaves* from Africa to toil and die in the mines, sending gold to Europe. To the wealthy. To the bullies and parasites.

The descendants of those African slaves, and the indigenous people, and the colonizers who enslaved them both, still live throughout these territories. Many of the countries and cities still bear the names—and languages—of Spain and Portugal.

But... They Didn't Introduce It

The enslaving and murder of the indigenous people groups of the "New World" was a horror and a capital crime of staggering proportions. The Europeans decimated the territories they invaded, and the people they used were innocent victims. But many of them were already enslaved before the conquistadors arrived.

Before Columbus "discovered" the Americas, there were extensive human populations. The continent was home to millions—*thousands* of tribes and civilizations throughout what we call South, Central and North America. Social organization ranged from family-style cultures to loose-knit cooperating neighboring tribes, to democracies, to large autocratic kingdoms and vast empires.

Slavery was common among the Mayan and Aztec empires—two cultures widely known today—but it also existed throughout the Americas. Long before Spain and Portugal invaded, the region had its own bullies and parasites: indigenous peoples who enslaved one another across rival tribes and empires. Europe didn't introduce slavery—but they industrialized it, making it more brutal and far-reaching.

Slavery In and From Africa

Recall the earlier quote from the King of Bonny (now Nigeria), in rejecting the British attempt to end the slave trade, who said the British "can never stop a trade ordained by God himself." He was evidencing a common practice throughout Africa—as it was also common throughout the world—of people enslaving their own families and their neighbors. They sold children to pay off debts. They captured men, women and children in conflicts with other tribes or villages. They sacrificed their own, and captives, to appease the gods or ensure a good crop. And they sold any and all of these to slave traders within their own continent, and from foreign sea-going powers like Spain, Portugal, France and Britain.

To be achingly clear: International slave-traders didn't raid inland or capture indigenous people all by themselves. They typically bought captives from local rulers and middlemen who had done the capturing—often profiting from the sale of their own kin or neighboring tribes. The logistics made it cheaper and safer to outsource the violence.

It was a supply chain: from captor to distributor to sales force to purchaser to end-user—just like any commodity today. Notably, the suppliers kept and used some of their own product: *Indigenous people enslaved other indigenous people.* People were just tools—and stored like tools, in the shed.

It was a *global* reality. On every continent, slavery was business as usual. When Britain moved to end the trade, the effort was mocked as naïve and impractical. Why dismantle something that was working so well?

And slavery like this still persists—we don't witness it personally, any more than the nobles in Europe witnessed the exploitation of the Native peoples on the other side of the world. Colonial expansion *then* is paralleled by economic parasitism *today*. We benefit because others, *out of sight*, are oppressed and exploited, *here* and abroad.

In the United States

Some Native American tribes—long before the mass colonization by Europeans—also practiced slavery, enslaving war captives. That doesn't excuse the brutal treatment, dispossession and murder Native peoples later suffered at the hands of colonizers. The actual history is ugly.

"Thanksgiving" conjures images of pilgrims and Indians peacefully dining together—and there was some truth to that. But the far greater story was a sustained and massive wave of immigration from Europe that resulted in the steady seizure of Indigenous land, and the forced displacement or slaughter of its inhabitants. Slavery wasn't the primary tool in this conquest; rather than being captured for labor, Native people were more often driven away or killed outright. By bullies.

There *was* slavery—but mostly of Africans, imported by British and other European slave traders. Slavery supported European farming, business and wealth-building, beginning during the Colonial Era (British, French, Spanish, Portuguese) and continuing after the War of Independence.

We unfortunately tend to associate American slavery with the South—plantations, auctions, enslaved Black families laboring under white masters—but it was embedded in the very fabric of the country, long before the official founding (i.e., while still a colony of Britain), and it was largely regarded much as Marcus Aurelius or Aristotle regarded it: a normative and unexceptional reality. Good business.

Most slave owners throughout history, including in early America, were actually oblivious to or willfully ignorant of the evil they were doing. It was rationalized, promoted, celebrated as the natural, God-ordained order of things. It helped grease the wheels of the human enterprise, subsidizing the wealthy, and helping even average free families. Why question what worked?

George Washington owned 124 slaves. Late in life, he grew uneasy with the practice, increasingly realizing its inhumanity and trying to find a "legal" solution (it was complicated). In his will he ultimately freed all of them after his and his wife's deaths. Thomas Jefferson owned some 600 slaves and fathered children by at least one, Sally Hemings.

It was common among the founders. We may recoil at this, or try to ignore, minimize or deny it, but **it was real**. And it was **wrong**.

In 1807, Britain outlawed the *slave trade*—but not slavery itself. That was the *beginning* of a realization that exploiting one group of humans to support the power, wealth and comfort of another is unjust. But that recognition must extend further—to include not just the obvious slaveries of history, but also the ones still hiding in plain sight.

Slavery was, and is, and is to come.

The Coal Mines of Appalachia

In 1947, Merle Travis wrote a song that struck a chord deep in the American working class. "Sixteen Tons" became a classic, especially after Tennessee Ernie Ford performed it on national television in 1956. It became his trademark:

> Some people say a man is made outta mud
> A poor man's made outta muscle and blood
> Muscle and blood and skin and bones
> A mind that's a-weak and a back that's strong
> You load sixteen tons, what do you get?
> Another day older and deeper in debt
> Saint Peter, don't you call me, 'cause I can't go
> I owe my soul to the company store.

The Appalachian Mountains stretch from Virginia to Alabama. Here's just one *illustrative sample* of slavery *hidden in plain sight* from one region of this mountain chain: the Scotch-Irish immigrants in West Virginia. They are "white people" from Scotland, Ireland and elsewhere who fled their home countries due to poverty and oppression. The hills and "hollers" (*hollows*, valleys) of West Virginia reminded them of home, and they settled in. It was a hard-scrabble life, but they made it work with farming, hunting, and crafts like weaving, pottery and furniture-making.

Then came *the mines*. Coal, the fuel of the railroads and industry, powered the country's westward expansion, so mining companies moved in and began digging. They hired locals to work the mines and built "company towns" to house the workers and their families. Miners were paid in company *scrip*—money valid only at the company store, the sole place in town to buy food, clothing, medicine, etc. The mining company also owned the homes and charged rent. If a miner's wages weren't enough to support his family—which was often—he went into debt to the store. Over time, workers became trapped in a closed system where every dollar earned circled right back to the company. When a miner died—common due to the dangerous working conditions (think accidents and black-lung disease)—his wife had seven days to marry another miner, or she and the children were evicted.

No one could afford to live on the salaries paid, so all the workers were in debt, had no savings or way to save, and what little they had was in company scrip anyway—which was worthless anywhere else.

Reread the song's lyrics. Recall what Aristotle said about slaves—people who exist only to be ruled. That's how the miners were seen: weak-minded, able-bodied, useful only for muscle and bones. Tools. They lived in company-owned shacks and died from accidents and black-lung. *Slaves*, kept without pity in chains made of debt, in wretched living conditions, whose lives subsidized the mine-owners' fortunes and powered the growth of the nation.

Eventually, unions began to organize. Their goal was to break the chains: better conditions, safer mines, and wages above destitution and servitude. But like Spartacus, the workers "didn't know their place." Their rebellion—such as the Battle of Blair Mountain—was violently crushed by company thugs and deputized "law" enforcement. Miners were murdered for their rebellion, for demanding freedom.

When we think of slavery in the United States, usually the only image that comes to mind are brown-skinned people kidnapped from Africa to work on Southern plantations. But white European immigrants were also brutalized—exploited, discarded, beaten or killed if they objected.

Slave owners don't much care what color their slaves are, and slavery takes many guises. It isn't an anomaly or rare exception. It's an awful, common reality. It's still right here, hiding in plain sight—even where you live.

Let me be clear: This book isn't attempting a thorough catalog of every form of slavery, everywhere, across all time. I'll provide links where you can explore that more deeply under *Slavery* in **Sources**. But my continuing point is that real slavery has existed, and exists *today*, in many forms and many places, and it is wrong. Morally *wrong*. And it's our responsibility to *see* it, *name* it, and *change* it. *And we can.*

Even so, we're not done yet:

Trafficking of "Domestic Servants"

America is hailed as "the land of the free and the home of the brave," a beacon of hope around the world for those fleeing poverty and oppression—just like early immigrants once did. They long for exactly the same thing: to escape from their awful circumstances and find opportunity, a fresh start, a new life.

But the bitter irony is this: Many of today's loudest opponents of immigration are themselves the descendants of immigrants who once sought—and received—*the very same chance*. Now that they're secure, they fight to keep others out. *"We've got ours, and we're not sharing!"*

Hopeful people fleeing poverty and oppression are exploited by the latest incarnation of slave traders: human traffickers. These parasites—the same ones who managed the slave trade—use boats, trucks and forced marches to move people across borders and into bondage. They move them from poor regions to wealthy buyers, in America and in nearly every other modern economy.

Their victims end up working in homes, on farms, in landscaping and factories. Some are forced into prostitution or crime—the brutal outcomes of having no other choice.

We've changed the labels. We get all huffy about "them" coming here—like *we* once did—and we either kick them out, or we turn around and use them anyway. The ones we let stay are used to subsidize our comfortable lifestyles.

It doesn't matter if you dislike this description. It is **true**.

To be clear, I'm not denigrating the jobs they do. I've done many of them myself. They're hard work and long hours. And the workers are typically paid well below minimum wage—off the books, in cash—and threatened with deportation if they dare complain. How is this not slavery?

And how do our rights to be here outweigh theirs? Because we got here first? Ask any Native American tribe about that idea. We've grown blind to the privileges of conquest and landownership.

If we are to enforce a standard of "legal" versus "illegal" immigration, it must rest on a moral foundation—not fear or self-interest. It must not be wielded as a bludgeon to keep others out. Yes, we need a thoughtful, compassionate approach to those fleeing oppression—alongside real protections from violent criminals. But blanket condemnation, hard borders and redlining the country don't meet *any* moral standard. We each need to examine ourselves and our motives in this. And ask, is this how *I* would wish to be treated, if *I had fled poverty* or *oppression* and come to this country for help and a new beginning?

Perhaps we need to begin remembering the Golden Rule, and apply it.

HIDDEN SLAVES TODAY – RETAIL SLAVERY

Bullies steal openly, because their power protects them. Parasites steal in hiding. But both are *thieves*—and often much worse.

We've seen slavery *in plain sight*: from Africans dragged across oceans to voluntary immigrants held captive by debt and thugs. But there are still others—slaves hidden from view, though their bondage is no less real.

Let's expose them now with a simple, iconic example, and the deceit that keeps it hidden. Think of it like that first spot of toxic mold you see on a wall. Soon you begin to see another. And another. And then you realize: It's everywhere.

Consider a modern retail clerk. Adjust the math as rates change—I show my work, sources and methods at **BPS.online** under *Retail Slaves*. The ratios will likely hold. They should horrify even the most callous person. The example that follows is actually relatively moderate, and not atypical. More extreme instances exist, but they're so outrageous that citing them here would create disbelief. You can hunt them down on your own—once you've seen this real-life example.

A major grocery chain in our middle-class neighborhood operates across many states. Its workers include supervisors, stockers, cleaners, cashiers and service clerks (baggers, cart wranglers). Clerks—usually the lowest-paid—make minimum wage even with a union and are capped at under 30 hours per week so the company can legally *avoid* providing health insurance (which averages about $6000 per year per person).

At the time of this writing, this grocery chain pays clerks about $17,000 per year at our state's unusually high minimum wage: **$15 per hour**.

That's more double the federal rate of **$7.25** (still used in most states). But let's stick with $15 per hour for our example.

The CEO of the same company makes **$14.5 million annually** in total compensation. He also receives a pension, paid vacation and excellent health insurance, of course. But let's consider just his income:

Economists assume the average year has 222 workdays (365 minus weekends, holidays and vacation). The average workday is eight hours.

Let's use these simple assumptions to calculate his hourly pay:

$14.5 million divided by 222 days is over **$65,000** *per day*—more than most people earn in a year.

$65,000 divided by 8 hours is just over **$8000 per hour**.

Let's be very plain:
- **The Master** (CEO) makes **$8000 per hour**.
- **The Slave** (clerk) makes **$15 per hour**.

Annually, the CEO makes **853 times** what the clerk does. This is wrong.

In one day, the CEO makes nearly **four times** what the clerk makes in **an entire year**. This is wrong.

The CEO has **excellent healthcare**, both to prevent disease and treat it when it occurs. The clerk gets **no healthcare**. This is wrong.

The CEO has **paid vacation, paid education and training benefits, paid travel for conferences and retreats, lavish working conditions** and **personal assistance**. The clerk has **none** of these. This is wrong.

The Master can buy a *really* **nice home** with a **few** *days* **of income**. The Slave can afford a **room in an apartment**, with not enough left over for food, clothing, transportation and healthcare. This is wrong.

Here's the severe truth: We've rebranded "master and slave" as "employer and employee," with slogans about working hard to get ahead. We celebrate the rare few whose talent, luck and hard work helped them rise up—as we should!—but for the countless working poor, it's still masters and slaves, disguised by masterful propaganda.

This is wrong. *It is slavery by any moral standard.*

Those who most benefit from this modern slavery might start to accuse this analysis as "Marxism," "socialism," "communism," "entitlement," "welfare," "nanny-state," "laziness," "sour grapes" and heaven knows what else. That's the rhetoric of fear and misdirection. It is *propaganda* that is meant to frighten us about any challenge to the social order.

Somehow the rich getting richer is a good thing, and the rest of us "benefit" from some sort of "trickle down" of wealth from those above us. The idea that the poor need more than table scraps is mischaracterized as "redistribution of wealth"—as if the poor are lazy parasites trying to rob the deserving rich. It is a lie that turns victims into villains—to keep us from seeing the truth of the profound injustice of today's hoarding of life-giving resources.

It is wrong.

WE SUBSIDIZE THEM

Any economic, corporate or legal system that holds you in your place, makes you a slave by underpaying you, while wealth flows upward. Robbed once, you've been mugged. But if bullies and parasites regularly take from you—your time, work, health and more—you are their slave. It is that simple.

There will be justifications, excuses, grand theories, misdirections, even laws to their benefit. As there are petty thieves and nation-stealers, so slavery ranges: from underpaid wage slaves to those in literal chains, beaten, broken and trapped by threat of death. *All* are slaves. Their lives, work, days, dignity, health, hopes and families—***stolen***.

While those in visible chains deserve our full efforts, focusing *only* on them blinds us to other, less-visible forms of slavery. Publicly decrying only on the worst cases **helps the system hide the others.**

Unless we deeply grasp the full extent of the ways and range of slavery—and the bullies and parasites who feed off us—we all will remain their literal slaves. *We* are the foundation and source of their wealth.

We subsidize them. They're our masters. This is reality, not hyperbole. It's time we realized this ugly fact and began to claim our lives and freedom.

The thieves will laugh at this claim. Or lie, distract or hide what they've taken. The very last thing they'll do—bully or parasite—is *let you* take it back. But you don't need their permission.

We'll see how to take it back, and we *will* take it back. Not by bloody revolution, or by using their cruelty as our tool. We don't need their permission. But don't jump ahead. First let's first fully grasp our reality:

We are slaves. Until we see the full, methodical evil of it—and its disguises—we'll be unable to stop it. We'll keep subsidizing the wealth and power of bullies and parasites.

To be clear, it's not about which job you hold or where you are. I grew up in a working-class neighborhood; we didn't have much money. I've worked since I was a kid, and I've had many kinds of jobs over the decades: picking trash, cleaning offices, shoveling snow, cutting grass, factory work, delivering newspapers, selling vacuums door-to-door, construction, mailman, retail clerk, musician, writer, engineer, city-services analyst, senior vice-president and CEO of national and international companies, and lastly pastor of a small, multi-ethnic church.

I've often joked that I've tried to pack as many lifetimes as I could into one. But one of the insights this has provided is of the fundamental equivalence of honest work, no matter what the job entails. The CEO of a major corporation is not more worthy than the clerk five levels down in the organization, nor the person who cleans the offices.

WHAT ABOUT PAY DIFFERENTIAL?

Rewarding higher levels of skill or responsibility isn't wrong, economically or ethically. It encourages excellence, education and accountability. What about the creative, dedicated entrepreneur, who strives and succeeds above and beyond the norm, and reaps the reward of that effort? All good things.

But is it *right*—morally or economically—that one person makes $15 per hour… and another $8000 *per hour*… in the same company, in the same country? Is it *right* that some are stuck in poverty and ill health while others live in luxury?

STUCK IN POVERTY? I DON'T BELIEVE IT.

Let's take a brief detour to consider the legal and social quicksand of those stuck in poverty. If we've never been up close to it, the indignities and inescapable shackles may be hard to see or even believe.

This is a true and *unexceptional* example. The name and place are changed to protect the innocent.

Pat is 33. She's only ever lived in a room of someone else's apartment. She's finished high school, but family hardships stopped her from going further. Like countless retail clerks, she's limited to part-time hours—no medical insurance, and not enough income to save anything at all. She has no bank account—and no idea how they work. Her employer pays her with a weekly debit gift card—a common method for low-wage workers.

One day Pat was arrested and jailed after a loud argument—on a false complaint. The charges were eventually dismissed, months later, but the consequences were severe. Her bail was $1000—not high for most of us. But she had no money, and no friends or family with that kind of money. It might as well have been a million. That's how the legal system traps the poor.

So she missed work without explanation—and lost her job.

With no income, she lost her sublet.

She had no lawyer. And no family member to get her one.

She was now caught in a months-long legal process, with no way out—even though the arrest should never have happened.

Unlike many of us who've watched legal dramas on TV, Pat didn't know that a lawyer could be appointed for her by the court—so she never asked. None was given.

Like so many, Pat was a hostage to poverty: poor, broke and now in jail. She didn't know what to do at all. No way out.

I heard about the arrest and went to visit. I went to a bank, got $1000 cash, and bailed her out. My little congregation put up the money for an attorney—a major effort for us. After many weeks of hearings, motions and expenses, all of the charges were dropped.

Pat was "free"—but broke, jobless and homeless. Dejected, lost, confused. Despite our best efforts, she ended up on the street, homeless. There, her wallet—and ID—was lost or stolen—common for the homeless.

She tried to find work, but without ID, she couldn't get hired. She was given a lift to the Secretary of State's office for a new ID—but they required identification to get one! They told her to bring a certified birth certificate and utility bills in her name.

She had no money to pay for the certificate, no way to get to the hospital, and no ID to prove she was the one legally requesting it.

She'd never had utility bills—she'd only ever rented a room in someone else's apartment. And even though the Secretary of State could easily pull up her old ID record, with her photo, and issue a new ID, they would not do it without proper ID and utility bills.

She considered joining the Navy. It would be a good way to escape her circumstances. At a recruiting office, she scored so high on the entrance exam that they were very interested in having her enlist immediately.

But she had no ID. And she was on prescribed medications for some psychological conditions—but the Navy doesn't accept anyone on any such medicines, even those legitimately prescribed.

A local shelter had the same medication ban. She was turned away.

She spent many nights on the street. Now she's in another shelter that was willing to take her in and might help her rebuild. We hope.

She has been so beaten down by this whole process—as have been some of us who have tried all along to help her—that she is now depressed, angry, hopeless and lacking the will to try again. She is stuck by despair—*and* by circumstances, regulations and social structures that seem to have no means of escape.

I don't share this story to ask for help. I share it because most people can't imagine how desperate life is when you're trapped in poverty. Working class, middle class, upper class—we have friends, family, bank accounts, knowledge and options. We can usually find a way out.

But from within our protective shells, we can't fathom how hard it is—or how few exits there are—for someone stuck in poverty. We can't imagine how miserable it is. We can't *see* it. And we don't *believe* it.

An average person from a middle-class family and culture may take an entry-level minimum wage job, attend college or trade school and move on to a steady career, with solid income, housing, savings, investments.

If they don't like the minimum-wage job they have, they can usually find another, and medical insurance is provided through the family or even the Affordable Care Act. They live with family or friends and navigate the basics of society, jobs and banking. Though it may be hard at times, fundamentally they are in a relatively safe place, protected by family and friends—and it all basically *works*.

For someone like Pat, it could not be more different. Even without the arrest, it just doesn't work. Without family or friends, there's no support network. No job options. No income to afford even a small apartment.

She ends up on the street not because she's lazy and irresponsible, but because society offers her no way out of her trap. She's *stuck*. Our society *works* for those already protected—even with challenges. But it *fails* for those at the bottom.

I've discovered that those of us who have never been stuck in poverty *simply cannot believe* how despairing, difficult, ugly and entangling it truly is. Even if you mean well—does this ugliness seem real to you yet?

For those stuck at the bottom, options are simply shut off.

There is no exit. No job without ID. No ID without ID. No job.

You may think this is simply a bizarre exception, but it's reality for millions of American citizens—and for many immigrants, legal or not.

And even when these marginalized folks manage to get a job, the very-low pay—without healthcare—means no savings, no education, no escape. They are stuck, shackled. *Slaves* by any other name.

More than 10% of our population—some 37 million people—live in poverty. Many suffer and die there, trapped by circumstance.

It's easy to think people just need to try harder and things will improve. But you and I need an *awakening*—to leave our insulated safety and *see* the inescapable misery, suffering and death that traps so many.

I don't mean to be harsh, but when I write elsewhere about

> **"neighbors who care for others just as they themselves desire to be cared for: in food, clothing, housing, healthcare, education and safety, and in the thriving community that results from that mutual care"**

… this can't just be a lifestyle tweak for the well-off. If we fail to care for those truly stuck, we endanger everyone's future—including our own children's. But if we ensure these things for everyone, our own futures become more abundant and assured. It really is simple.

So, to ask the difficult question again:

Is it morally and economically right that one person makes $15 per hour and the other $8000 per hour, in the same company, in the same country? That some remain in poverty and ill health while others live in luxury?

No. It is *wrong*. If in our wildest imaginings we think this is a good thing—somehow an essential part of the success of an economic system like capitalism—then propaganda works. We have accepted slavery as a "higher good" that supports—*subsidizes*—the bullies.

If mutual care sounds wild-eyed, radical, Marxist, socialist or communist—then propaganda works. That's how the lie survives.

It is perfectly right and just to criticize and oppose oppressive "communist" regimes anywhere in the world. Of course. They are led by bullies and parasites, and their people are slaves to the regimes and subsidize their masters. All true.

But it is *also* true that our "free-enterprise capitalist democracy" has the same problem: Some rise by holding others down. Our system keeps some held down, subsidizing those above them. Some are stuck in poverty and are powerless to escape it.

These conditions will not be easy to change. It is a powerful and extensive system in which we are all caught up. But we will remain chained if we accept the chains as moral or necessary. They are neither.

Only when we *see* the slavery, and the lies that sustain it—as wrenching as the discovery may be—can we begin to break the chains.

And the problem isn't capitalism itself. It's the bullies and parasites who manipulate, twist and exploit *any* system. It is their thefts, and their defenders, the *propagandists*.

We need to subject their lies to rigorous analysis. And not be tricked into thinking mutual care is some kind of communist conspiracy.

Are we that gullible?

PROPAGANDA

Fear is virtually always the vulnerability that bullies and parasites use to manipulate us to do their will. One of their key methods is *propaganda*. The word is thrown around in political debate so often that it barely even registers anymore. It's just another word for "lie." People in power lie to stay in power. So what? That's not a surprise. It's become background noise. We ignore it and get on with our lives.

And if we are really caught up in some giant scheme or "matrix" to enslave us and force us to subsidize the bullies and parasites above us—as this book alleges—wouldn't that be obvious? *Really obvious*?

Nope. It's *not* obvious. That's the point. Propaganda *does* work.

When our lives are ruled by bullies and parasites, it is often well-crafted lies that hold us in our place. Propaganda is cheaper than violence.

If you believe you're in an inescapable prison, guards are hardly needed. If you don't even *know* it's a prison, even less so. So let's see why propaganda works…

In some countries, baby elephants in captivity are chained by one leg and prodded with a sharp metal rod—and taught unrelentingly to do the bidding of their human trainers. As adults, they are used to haul heavy loads, transport people or goods, or perform for entertainment.

Elephants are highly intelligent—they have five times more neurons than humans—and can learn many complex skills for work or for show. Yet in adulthood, they obey the tiny humans who trained them, because since birth, they believe humans are more powerful. So the elephants remain compliant. They remain bound by the *very same chain* from childhood. They could snap it easily—but they *believe* it still holds them.

We humans are no wiser than elephants here. We could snap the chains and walk free—out of the doorless prisons we thought held us—*if* we stopped believing the lies that keep us in our place.

KINDS OF LIES

Some lies serve good ends—like hiding an innocent person from a vicious mob: "He ran down that alley over there." Other lies conceal wrongdoing: "I didn't steal the wallet—I found it on the sidewalk." Or: "I was just following orders."

We all know these things. Lies come in many forms. Most of us have told or heard one—maybe even in the last hour. They're everywhere every day: in the press, on the Internet and social media, on podcasts, radio and television, in ads and politics, in friends and families, at work, home, stores, online and offline. We *swim* in lies.

Lies are so persistent that our brains tune out all but the most glaring. Even those we often shrug off—or worse, fall down a rabbit hole of imagined conspiracies. Propaganda's emotional appeal—fear, hope, outrage—make it powerful. It flatters, simplifies, justifies, all to hide the lies. It relies upon repetition, false dichotomies, slogans, scapegoating, sugarcoating, appeals to tradition.

And here's the danger: The most insidious lies hide in plain sight. We've been made blind to lies. That's the essence of effective propaganda: Its power is that we can't see it at work.

Most of us lie on impulse—to avoid embarrassment or get ahead. Propaganda is different: planned, orchestrated and manipulative, and wielded by bullies along with intimidation, cruelty and secrecy. And even if we know it is there—especially from "our side," we often choose to be voluntarily complicit in its propagation.

Propaganda is the Big Lie—a "long con." It survives by piling up a thousand smaller lies and *helpers* that create the illusion of truth. It's a manufactured "reality," a fiction where you play a part.

In *As You Like It*, Shakespeare wrote, "All the world's a stage, and all the men and women merely players." That's always been true, but when you're a victim of propaganda, it's worse—you're cast as an unwitting player in someone else's fiction, and you pay to perform.

Perhaps it's time to quit our part in the play.

ALL THE PLACES PROPAGANDA LIVES AND WORKS

(True examples of each can be found in **Sources**, under *Propaganda*.)

Financial Scams

Financial scammers create illusions of wealth and success—flashy cars, expensive clothes, expensive homes and large, impressive offices. Others go the opposite route: modest, tasteful offices with credentials on the wall, like those of a trusty financial advisor.

They're often warm and personable—seeming to care about you, your family, your needs and fears. That trustworthy persona numbs your instincts, your critical thinking, and lulls you into handing over your savings, your home, your investments. The papers they have you sign make it all seem legitimate, but they really exist to protect them should you try to recover what you gave them.

They draw in victims with dreams of escape from depressing conditions or promises of future luxury or security. Your money goes to them now, with huge "gains" promised later. They never come. You may get regular reports showing your initial investment and its steady growth. You don't want to withdraw any of it, because the gains feel so regular and comforting! You may even be allowed to withdraw small amounts when needed—to keep your confidence up and your money in "the fund." But the reports are fake, just ink on paper or pixels on a screen, and your actual money is long gone—hidden in other bank accounts, or used to buy the cars, homes, watches, jewelry, yachts and other properties for your fund manager… and to make him or her seem more credible to the next mark.

In Ponzi schemes, Golden Circles or Multi-Level-Marketing (MLM) versions of this con, you're even recruited to draw in new investors. Earlier members are paid with the new investors' money, making it all *seem* like it is all working. But no real wealth is created, and no real investment growth happens. It's an illusion—manufactured to keep new money coming in. Propaganda in its simplest form.

These scammers range from local social acquaintances and friends to Wall Street titans, and their victims range from the working poor to huge charities, institutions and wealthy families. Even local and national governments have been taken by these parasites! The rule of thumb here is always, "If it seems too good to be true, it probably is." And if someone says, "I know this seems too good to be true, but…", assume you're about to be scammed. (Again, real examples in ***Sources***.)

Cults

No cult believes it is a cult. Instead, they *know* that their way is the *only* way, and *all others* are against them and must be avoided, defeated or even killed. True believers defend their leaders and won't even consider other voices. Your time, work and income support the cult—and its leaders, who live better than you. That difference, they say, is a sign of their genius, or holiness, or need—or a "hopeful example" to you.

We tend to think of cults as religious, but many have no religious pretense. In form and substance, what they share is fear or hatred of outsiders, blind loyalty to an idea or ideal, and worship of idealized leaders. There are movements and countries today just like this. Is mine like this? Is yours? We have to be willing to look. They're built on propaganda.

Blasphemy, Apostasy, Heresy

Blasphemy? Apostasy? Heresy? We usually hear those accusations made against someone who speaks against—or is accused of offending—a religious leader, founder or theology. Or a god, or ancestors, or an idea.

In rigidly controlled societies—especially where the leader is regarded as divine, or as God's appointed master—it often leads to the death penalty, or at a minimum to shunning, banishment or prison.

Are there bad ideas that should be confronted? Of course. But the real disorder is how bullies and parasites react when their "right" to rule or steal is questioned. Their propaganda defines you as the outlaw.

For not respecting, for writing or speaking words that threaten their sacred or social worldview—and hence their position above you—you are silenced, jailed or even killed.

This really is a most extreme and obvious predatory response to the least-violent kind of opposition: speaking out. But "the pen is mightier than the sword," and bullies know it.

Silencing opposition protects the powerful. But... *the open exchange of ideas—the battle of wits, the swirl of abuse and insight, of success and failure—is less secure, less consistent, less complete. And yet more true.*

In plain prose: Free speech is much more difficult, and costly. But actual truth depends on it.

Conspiracy Theories

No conspiracy *believers* think their theories are mistaken. Their fears and suspicions become their reality. Even the absence of evidence becomes proof of how good their foes are at hiding the truth. Every event is interpreted to affirm their grave suspicions.

They connect the dots compulsively, inventing false narratives that intentionally twist facts to the benefit of a few—and feed on the fears of many. (See especially *Fear of the Other* in **Sources**.)

These theories often rely on two yoked flaws. First is *false authority*—someone posing as an expert who actually isn't. An authority figure gives an "expert opinion." Here's where the second flaw comes in, *topic ignorance*—where listeners don't know enough to realize the so-called "expert" isn't one *on this topic*. The listeners' ignorance keeps them from discerning the fraud. The blind being led by the blind, if you will.

Statistics

Mark Twain once said, "There are three kinds of lies: lies, damned lies, and statistics." All of us have a gut sense that some statistics—especially those used to prove a point—are suspect, misleading or even intentional lies meant to manipulate us. One of the most common and least-recognized of these is confusing *correlation* with *causation*, thinking that because things happened at about the same time or place, one caused the other. (See *Exposing Statistical Tricks and Errors* in **Sources** for more.)

This becomes a very dangerous problem, especially when bullies and parasites exploit our ignorance for their benefit. They structure their propaganda to belittle those who dissent, and they trot out fake studies or distort real ones—all to keep us trapped and compliant. And of course, they will hotly deny that theirs is a "conspiracy theory." (Again, examples and more in **Sources**.)

Astute readers are likely now thinking, *Wait a minute! This whole idea about us as slaves subsidizing and defending our masters and the system without our knowing it—isn't this just another conspiracy theory?*

If I wanted to brush off the whole premise of *Bullies, Parasites and Slaves*, that's what I'd say. Which is why, at the very start, I said: "I need to prove it." The illustrations, sources, methods, examples and histories are all available—to substantiate these claims, and to help us see our dystopian reality enough to change it. And encourage each other.

And create mutual care.

Despots

From local committee members to national leaders, political bullies cast visions of threat and opportunity, and themselves as the only means to defeat the first and seize the second. They praise supporters and dehumanize or punish dissenters. Swagger, exaggeration and imagined moral superiority fuel the demonizing of "the other side." At the extremes, violence—even genocide—is justified and praised, though it's all rooted in lies, repeated lies and propaganda. You pay for their power—through taxes, conscription, fines for wrong beliefs or actions, and are forced to defend their actions, even if you don't agree.

It's Everywhere!

But it's not just political—it's cultural, commercial, personal. Religion, science, business, medicine, social groups, finances, family, education, psychology, law, politics—these are a few of the places where there are bullies and parasites for whom propaganda is vital—because it works—and why we *must* learn to recognize propaganda—because that's the only way to resist it.

Not seeing it comes at a cost. So, take time—real, intentional time—to reflect on some of the lies and propaganda you've personally seen or lived. In your social, religious and political circles. In school, online, on TV. In the news. In shopping: Think of the shaming of fashion failures, and the power of "influencers" and peer pressure, or the price you paid for that watch. And in celebrity: How we look up to fame and indulge in idol worship.

Propaganda is a helpful label, but it hides itself under less-obvious efforts, like PR, advertising and publicity. They're often attractive, self-flattering campaigns to get us to buy, believe or act—for *someone else's benefit*. At the very least, we should question the motives behind the bragging—and the damage it can cause to the audience.

Years ago, I worked as a recording engineer for a Los Angeles record-production and management company. One of their bands was becoming quite popular. I toured with them and watched as the number of fans grew and became increasingly attracted by their music and fame. Groupies were everywhere and swarmed the band members after every concert. The production company fed this relentlessly with press releases about the band's genius and innovative music.

The guys in the band began to get a bit full of themselves, and swagger and attitude began to show. They had risen from a hard-working local club band but were now famous and getting more so.

Their managers called a meeting. I was there. They sat the band members down in the office, talked with them about their recent successes and fame, and said, "Guys, listen to us: Don't believe your own publicity!"

Their managers, who had nurtured and coached and publicized them through years of hard work and praise-filled press releases, punctured their pride balloon and made it real, saying in effect: "We bragged about you to promote you and to make money for all of us. It's what we do to sell records. Don't believe the hype. It's *hype*. You're good musicians, but not high-and-mighty music gods and worthy of all praise. Get over yourselves, and get back to work making music. We'll brag about you. But don't believe it yourselves. Lose the attitude!"

It worked. They continued to make good music and good money, but lost the swagger. I tell this story to illustrate this point: Propaganda comes in many forms. It's a shape-shifter. But its goal is always the same: to manipulate us to do or believe something for the benefit of someone else.

Watch for it. That's just one industry—but it works the same way everywhere. Recognizing it may be a miserable awakening, but it sharpens our insights and strengthens our resistance. And when we're not being drained by being tricked, we are more able to care for each other.

Keeping Us In Our Place

Propaganda is almost always a lie camouflaged with truths and apparent truths. Its purpose is to keep us in our place, distracted and unaware that others are feeding off us. Learning to recognize its forms and methods is key to freeing ourselves—from propaganda, and from those who use it.

Keep looking for it! Rip off the pretty bandage, probe the seeping wound, and you'll see the parasites within. Flush them out and healing can begin.

Remember: Bullies take because they can—openly, when they have power and are willing to intimidate or harm, or just for perverse pleasure. Parasites steal more subtly—hiding their theft through deception or numbing.

Both employ propaganda to preserve their ongoing thefts. Even their self-glorifying biographies and publicity are a form of propaganda—though they often come to believe their own lies.

Palace Guards

"Palace guards" are the *defenders of privilege*—whether actual soldiers, a police force, media personalities or institutional leaders. Their roles earn them honor and reward from those in power—to help keep them in power. They're the ones that praise and defend the glorious leader and suppress or ridicule any opposing voices.

Palace guards work to ensure the continuation of oppression and unequal care, and propaganda is cheaper than most other methods of guarding the palace. It is therefore well-planned, thorough, convincing and accepted as "reality." Its authors are gifted persuaders. It will only fail if we learn to recognize it and resist its disguises and seductions.

The tools and means that should be used to protect all of us are twisted to guard those who steal and hoard. What should preserve the common good and guard mutual care is deployed to protect the predators.

Chess and War

In chess, the first into battle and the first to die are the pawns. The King and Queen stand behind, protected by knights and bishops. This should explain most everything about how monarchies are ordered, who is sacrificed, and how bullies protect themselves. To them it is just chess, after all. Those who have died may be honored with portraits and medals, but they are still dead. We are pieces on their gameboard, and after our deaths they commission the stories of their own genius and glory.

Pick a war, any war, at any time in history, and you will find soldiers and advocates on every side who truly believe their sacrifices are good and just. There will be mercenaries who don't care, of course. But whether it is saving democracy or advancing an empire, advancing a religion or fighting off evil bullies and regimes, there will be people on both sides who believe what they are doing is right.

A distant observer would clearly see the difference: those struggling to fulfill mutual care versus the ones hoping to take what is not theirs.

Time and distance allow such a sane analysis, but the passion and noise of any current battle makes it vastly more difficult. In our own world today, there are those that call the other side the "Great Satan" and are called the "Axis of Evil" by their opponents. Both sides demonize the other. It is an effective, ancient propaganda technique that makes the murder of your foe seem just and right.

Here some readers are thinking, *So then everyone is evil or unwittingly defending something evil? Or everyone thinks they are protecting all that is good? Is our human life just predator, prey and propaganda after all?*

This is cynical, but not wrong. If we are to move beyond this ancient horror, we must recognize its promoters and resist them. When those who profit from war—either bullies or parasites—are able to *make a profit* by attacking others, or pretending to defend us, *they will*. When they are in a position to make war happen, war will happen.

Bullies take because they can. Parasites profit by manufacturing destruction. We *must* defend against bullies—foreign or domestic—but we've often failed to distinguish true threats from invented ones, reality from propaganda. *We can learn how to know the difference*. It will take courage, insight and hard work.

Collateral Damage

Bullies and their supporters might not approve of every act of cruelty, murder, theft, enslavement, or death of innocents who happened to be near their target—but in their minds they accept it as a "necessary evil" to accomplish a "higher good." The euphemism "collateral damage" is often invoked to minimize the murders of others who just happened to be near their primary target.

When these decisions are made, the expression is commonly heard, "We're the adults in the room. We do what we must." Those who oppose such decisions as *immoral* are dismissed as *naïve*.

Soldiers are trained to accept this as an unfortunate part of war. And with weapons and missiles that work at a distance, it's easier to ignore the murder of innocents. You don't have to see face-to-face those who you are killing—neither your intended target nor those other men, women and children who were simply nearby.

Even worse, there are some who *enjoy* the deaths of *any* others in the advance of their own ambitions. You have heard their own words.

Worse still, bullies in war often *calculate* the murder of civilians—innocent people—to "weaken the will" of their opponents. It is a most cynical evil, and soldiers are sent to war with mind-numbing propaganda that lets them commit just such horror—though soldiers who survive later pay the price in psychological trauma.

This killing of innocents is the primary method of "terrorists," but it is used and excused by all sides. Treaties like the Geneva Convention have tried to ban such tactics. Our best hopes might imagine a day when they have ended. But they persist—because bullies use force to do their will. They take because they can. Right and wrong are not considered, unless necessary to preserve their power and takings. Propaganda is employed to make it all seem right.

I pray we comprehend the depths of this depravity. And hate it enough to change it. *Will we learn to see through it—and refuse to play along?*

PART 2: THE SOLUTION

How do we practically build a civilization based on mutual care?

What are the foundations, rules, methods, insights and practical skills to make it actually work?

The chapters to follow will set the foundations in place: our shared insights, skills, *moral standards*, hope and work.

We *can* make it happen.

OVERCOMING PRIDE AND FEAR

Pride and fear are *both* barriers to mutual care, and *if mutual care is our goal*, which is surely must be, then we need to first comprehend how these two common and related emotions can keep us from it. Bullies and parasites use both of them to maintain their positions and keep us in our places. Let's rob them of these weapons. Consider…

Many people and groups still regard themselves or their "race" as superior—sometimes with overt, swaggering pride; sometimes simply as a quiet fear of the other: a deep unease with people or cultures who are unfamiliar to us or don't look like us. And so we imagine ourselves as better than them. We are proud of *us*, and we fear *them*.

The words *race* and *racism* are so familiar in our vocabulary and in public debate that few realize that "race" itself is a highly suspect category. In the 19th century, one idea was that humanity could be neatly divided into categories like Caucasian, Negroid, Asian and so on. That idea is highly inaccurate, unscientific, and unhelpful—and it does not reflect the enormous diversity of shapes, sizes and colors that humans inhabit.

This error has also helped fuel nonsense theories about a master race, eugenics, and the evolution of an Apex Predator. More at *Master Races* in **Sources** at **BPS.online**.

The truth is, we're all mutts. Whatever you look like, your ancestors came from a long line of mixed skin tones, cultures, territories and worldwide emigrations—going back hundreds of thousands of years. Your ancestors mixed and matched. Abundantly. Really, they did.

My own ancestry (from both recent genealogy and genetics) is German, Polish, Ukrainian, Swedish, Norwegian and Scotch-Irish. Yet I share DNA with (among a host of others) a small Jewish remnant in Sardinia, and Israel, and Samaritans, and the Maasai tribe in East Africa. I'm a mutt.

I'm pink and a bit under average height in my country. The Maasai are brown and tall. As I age, I'm getting shorter—and I've noticed little brown spots appearing here and there. Maybe my Maasai ancestry is asserting itself. Could it *please* make me a little *taller*?

I'm a mutt—and so are you. Any pretentions about racial purity or a "master race" are pure bunk. They collapse under even the most basic scientific or historical scrutiny. For all the proclamations and rants some make about "preserving the white race" (or Aryan, Asian, African or any other), such notions are without foundation in genetics or genealogy.

There is no master race. No sub-human race. There is no "pure" line of ancestry or DNA anywhere. We are each a complicated, complex stew of history and human wanderings.

PRIVILEGE

Sadly, we've taken vast human diversity and boiled it down into a handful of vague categories—then used those to defend privilege. It's that simple.

Here's one example from my life—to help you reflect on your own.

I grew up in a completely white suburb of Chicago. I didn't know a single person with dark skin. I don't think I'd so much as encountered anyone who didn't look like me, even in a store. It never even occurred to me. I had no prejudice, but also no experience, or any reason to even think about race or inequality. It just didn't come up.

In Sunday School we were taught a little song…

> Jesus loves the little children,
> All the children of the world;
> Red and yellow, black and white,
> All are precious in His sight,
> Jesus loves the little children of the world.

Written shortly after the Civil War by Clarence Herbert Woolston, there are indications that the war provided some of the inspiration for it, but we knew none of this. We just learned and sang the song.

It made a deep and lasting impression on me. I understood: Skin color has nothing to do with our preciousness, our value. We are one—fundamentally, unshakably, indelibly.

By the time I reached high school, I'd become aware of race. Neighbors and relatives used words that repulse me today. They spoke of "negroes" as if they were *other*. *"They"* were "jungle bunnies" and "stove pipes" who played "jungle music" and lived in the ghetto by choice, in filth—lazy, showy, dangerous, because *"they"* didn't care, but *"they"* drove big Cadillacs to "show off." Everyone just knew that these things about them were true. *"They"* were not like *us*.

A very few of *"them"* began buying homes in the suburbs. It was a small number because those "niggers" were largely locked into jobs with low pay and little opportunity. This was an "invasion." It was a "dark wave" that would lower home values. They would turn our safe little town into a crime-riddled ghetto, endangering our lives, children, possessions and moral values. Some of *"them"* might even marry our daughters—or get them pregnant. *Miscegenation!*

Those really were the words and fears that gripped the neighborhood and kept people awake at night, fueled by hot rhetoric in public discourse and the press. And it's exactly like our world today: Immigrant invasions are the criminal swarms of our nightmares.

For today's politicians, just swap some nouns and locations in the paragraphs above.

Our *fear of the other* is still manipulated by bullies and parasites to preserve their positions of wealth and power. Here's how they did it then: "white flight" began the moment "they" moved near "us." A home on a block would be purchased by a "colored" family, and some parasitic realtors would go door-to-door, warning the neighbors to sell—fast. The value of their home was about to drop. So, houses sold rapidly as the worst fears were realized. Fear confirmed itself. Values dropped. Banks, investors and homeowners lost money, and realtors prospered.

The simple solution for the banks: Stop lending to negroes trying to buy homes in white neighborhoods. The banks took maps of the city and the surrounding suburbs and drew literal red lines around the areas they wanted to protect, and then prohibited mortgage loans to negroes.

This red-lining can be found in loan and home-sale documents from that time (actually beginning decades earlier), restricting purchases to the "Caucasian" race. I've even found it recently in the contract for local gravesites that my parents purchased when my siblings and I were kids. (More about the *History of Redlining* in **Sources**.)

I became aware of this horror, and joined the Civil Rights Movement in the '60s—based on what I'd seen and heard around me and in the press, and an inner sense that it was wrong to treat people badly just because they looked different or came from somewhere else.

So, thinking I was fulfilling a basic imperative of my faith—buoyed by the Reverend Dr Martin Luther King, Jr—I joined the NAACP and went to volunteer in its Community Action Project (CAP), an education, housing, economic and job-training program in inner-city Chicago.

It was an eye-opening experience, and a key to my insistent theme of mutual care throughout this book. The head of the CAP realized how naïve and nervous I was about the realities of the inner city and the people who lived there. Looking back, I suspect I hoped for the best but carried the fears of my all-white neighborhood somewhere in my mind and heart. He saw that my heart was in the right place—but that I didn't *get it* yet.

So he took me in hand and said, "There's someone I want you to meet." We walked a couple of blocks, up three flights of stairs, and he knocked on an apartment door. A pleasant African-American woman greeted us, invited us in, introductions were made, and we sat to chat.

I honestly don't recall what we talked about, but what made a lasting impression on me were the three young kids running around the apartment, playing with toys, and a children's show on the TV.

This was *my mom*! Or it could have been. And these were *us three kids*! Or it could have been.

I got it. The little song I'd learned in Sunday School was real here, and true. We were *the same*, and indelibly precious.

How could anyone, ever, anywhere, look down on and dismiss other members of the same human race? It was wrong. Foolish. I got it.

Now I needed to share that extraordinary insight with everybody else—friends, family, my local church members … in my all-white town.

I asked the (Black) man who ran this program if he'd be willing to come out to my suburban church and share what we were doing in the Community Action Project—job training, education and economic development for any inner-city residents—for poor Black families, certainly, but really for anyone regardless of ethnic background or previous struggles. It was a good thing, elevating many against great odds. *It was a story that needed to be heard!*

I went to my pastor, Lester Dacken, and asked him if I could invite this man, giving full details of who and what he and the program were, and he gave me permission to set up a talk at the church for an upcoming evening. I put up posters on the church walls and handed out flyers about it, at church and at the local college.

I was jazzed. Everyone would learn about the inner-city families, *love* what we were doing, and might want to be a part of it! Hooray! Yay team!

Opposition erupted immediately. Angry. Hot. Angry members organized a congregational meeting, and half the congregation voted to resign and leave the church if "that black man" was allowed in the building!

Many called him a communist because he worked for the NAACP. One man said he would wrap himself in an American flag and lie on the front porch of the church so *that man* would have to step on him *and the flag* to get into the building.

My naïveté about our pleasant, all-white neighborhood and my nice, fellow church members was shredded by their bitter, hateful words.

I was young, inexperienced, stunned and utterly at a loss.

I went to see Pastor Dacken. He had never been "political," nor involved (to my knowledge) in specific social causes or programs. He wasn't a "liberal" or "social gospel" preacher.

He simply looked after his flock. He taught about who Jesus was, what He *did* and *said*, and what He *urged* his followers to do. To Pastor Dacken, this was always the good news, the *gospel*: the God-commanded obligation to love each other. He lived it with his flock and preached on it week after week. *That* was Pastor Dacken.

And now I'd made a rippin' mess of his church.

I was crushed and felt awful, especially for him. Some brash young kid—me—had tried something new and "socially progressive," and now the whole church was coming apart at the seams, half ready to leave if that kid got his way! *Me.*

I apologized and offered to cancel the talk. That wise Black man and information about his inner-city program to help poor families would have to be canceled. *Damn.*

Once again came a life-changing moment. Pastor Dacken said, "George, you have understood the gospel. They have not. Even if I lose half of my congregation, you may have the talk here as planned."

I was grateful, overwhelmed, stunned. But more than anything, I was face-to-face with a man of true integrity, who did what was right regardless of the personal cost. What a privilege it was to know him, and to learn this lesson from his faith and courage.

I learned integrity from this. I'd like to say it strengthened my faith. But it didn't. I moved the talk to the local college, and I walked away from the faith and Christians.

I was sad more than anything. I thought I was on a team with others who believed in doing what Jesus taught: loving neighbors and even enemies, treating others as we want to be treated, helping those who are despised or not like us, and aiding those who are ill, or poor, or in jail.

Instead, I discovered that fully half of our congregation not only wasn't on that team, they actually despised and feared those Jesus told us to love. They bitterly attacked a wonderful man they'd never met who was coming to share about the caring work of the CAP in the inner city.

My honest thought at the time was, *If these Christians don't get it, who will?* I resolved to remain socially and politically active, but I stopped going to church or trusting it. I quit that team (foolishly, including the half that hadn't threatened to leave!)

Even so, years later, when I was arrested for protesting the Vietnam War, and my family couldn't afford bail, Pastor Dacken stepped in again—he gave me the money to get out. He *lived* it. He remains a blessed memory to me to this day.

Decades have passed. But there's been little moral progress in our country or the world. The labels have shifted. The groups of people we're afraid of have shifted. The fear remains—the *fear of the other*. We still don't know how to love those who are not like us. So the old system survives.

THE PREDATORY HIERARCHY

So, we can stay inside the predatory hierarchy—clinging to our place in the pecking order, hoping not to fall, and continuing in our *fear of others* to subsidize the bullies above us—those who exploit others, who steal and hoard, and whom we've allowed to rule.

Or we can resist—and choose mutual care instead. Resisting begins with refusing the lies, seeing others clearly. We can choose to be the team that works relentlessly toward mutual care, where abundance and thriving become the norm, where we share rather than hoard, and help each person grow and thrive. Where we ensure each other's food, shelter, clothing, health, education and safety, because it's morally right, and *wise*.

Mutual care works better than hoarding. It is the *wisdom* of loving. When we guarantee mutual care for all, abundance is the natural result. But we must *choose* the better way, and do it.

There will be fearmongering. You'll be called naïve, foolish, told horror stories of failed utopias—propaganda to protect those "above" you. Reject it.

Even the most frightened and bedraggled of us can learn to love and be loved. It works far better than the rule of bullies and parasites, the battles of thieves, the true dystopia.

Even so, it will be long, hard work, to undo the grip of those in power on the lives of those they keep in servitude and exploitation.

But it is possible. Let's start with this example:

BANNING THE SLAVE TRADE

As noted earlier, the British Empire ran the ships, logistics and business of trafficking human beings—mainly from Africa to the West, with eager collaboration from national and tribal bully rulers in Africa, and ready merchants and buyers in the West. Slavery was already ancient in Africa, as in most of the world throughout history, and those who profited from it defended it as normal and just. You can read factual accounts in *The Defense of Slavery* and opposing views in *Abolitionists*, both in **Sources**.

The push for real change began with Thomas Clarkson, Granville Sharp and several others, along with William Wilberforce, a member of the British Parliament. After a religious conversion, and the conviction that all should be loved equally (the Golden Rule), he recognized the horror of the slave trade, and so he introduced legislation in Parliament to outlaw it. It faced fierce opposition—selling humans brought wealth to Britain, especially to those with power and influence in Parliament, virtually all of whom professed to be Christians.

But to them, to stop slavery would be madness! The economy and our families would suffer from such foolishness! But like Lester Dacken, two centuries later, we could say of the Abolitionists: "You have understood the gospel. They have not."

Undeterred, Wilberforce reintroduced the same bill every year for 11 years. Over those years, and in the decades before them, leading up to his efforts in Parliament, he and his fellow believers crisscrossed Britain relentlessly, speaking out against the evil they saw, and persuading ordinary citizens that the buying and selling and owning of human beings was morally wrong—no matter how profitable.

The tide turned. Britain gained a conscience—rising up from ordinary people who saw evil and opposed it. The bullies and the parasites were outvoted, and after years of activism, finally the legislation passed.

The slave trade was made illegal and banned for British businesses in 1807. This did not stop slavery itself, in Britain or elsewhere. But in the U.S. it began a lengthy process that led to the American Civil War,

Lincoln's *Emancipation Proclamation* of 1863, the freeing of three and a half million American slaves, and even to the Civil Rights Act of 1964.

The process has been very long and difficult. But through persistence—Wilberforce's example, and a growing movement of like-minded allies over centuries—we've seen real change. Not finished. But real.

Yet much remains. We still benefit from systems built on the marginalization of others. And we'll only break from that legacy when we clearly see this: True *mutual care* is imperative not just because it is morally right, but because it also fosters abundance and thriving for all, when all are well-cared for and able to be their best selves: housed, healthy, well-fed, educated, safe. Loved.

"A rising tide lifts all boats" is true when all, and especially the poorest, are lifted. It is a lie when only the rich are getting richer, and only the comfortable are comforted.

The true rising tide is produced when all contribute, and all benefit.

JOINING CARE WITH WISDOM

Mutual care means sharing resources, rights and responsibilities across the whole community. This is where outrage gives way to wisdom—wisdom about how to end human exploitation, with *practical intelligence*, not just good-heartedness.

Let's set some foundations. These foundations will shape everything that follows—especially the design of a better future.

For all their bragging and self-promotion, bullies can't justify their theft, hoarding, harm, cruelty and murder. Whether it's the schoolyard bully stealing lunch money. Or the politician—or mob boss—sending out lackeys to extort and defraud. The scammer who smiles while stealing someone's life savings. The CEO who pads his pay by underpaying his staff and denying benefits. The insurance executive who denies lifesaving care to boost profits. The pharmaceutical giant that charges thousands for essential medicines. None can justify what they do.

Nor can those who traffic, rape and abuse the poor and powerless, or those who hoard the world's resources—land, water, food, medicine, fuel, shelter, power or truth. Those who murder by war or by policy. Conquerors who murder other human beings for wealth or power.

Bullies and parasites can offer no justification for their wickedness, because there is none. There never was. There never can be. They've tried. Excuses, lies, misdirection, bribes, spectacle. But none of it justifies what they do—steal, harm and kill.

On the other hand—throughout history—there have been those who saw a different way. Who realized that *mutual care* is the best creator and guarantor of the future. Even when far-removed in culture or time, with no awareness of one another, these rare, great minds illumined the lives around them with the same truth. Their insight endures. Their lives light the way through the darkness of a world captive to selfishness, hoarding and theft. Across languages, cultures, thoughts and faiths, they all taught the same simple truth. For these philosophers of the heart, their message was one:

Mutual care creates thriving and abundance. It is the way of wisdom.

Some were scorned, cast aside, even killed. Others were praised and revered—only to be ignored by those who claimed to follow them. Yet their insight remains. It's not difficult. Not obscure. Not lost. They pointed toward the wisdom of loving. Let their light illuminate us now.

THE LOVING OF WISDOM

Philosophy often gets a bad rap. We imagine professors lost in thought, arguments that never end or abstract ideas that don't touch the real world. But the word "philosophy" itself offers something clearer, more grounded, more essential—if we pay attention to its roots. It isn't just abstract talk. At its core, it means something simple and human: love of wisdom. The word "philosophy" comes from two Greek terms: *philo* and *sophia*. The pairing exists in some form across every language and culture. But these Greek words can help us uncover something profound. This insight—the joining of love and wisdom—appears relentlessly across geography and time, from prophets to poets to practical guides.

Let's break it down.

Philo means love—not romantic desire, not passing affection, but the kind of enduring love we feel for family and those we call our own. Parents, children, siblings, even aunts, uncles, cousins, lifelong friends. It is the willingness to care for and protect someone because *they are yours* and *you are theirs*. It's more than just emotion alone; it's action-based: doing what's needed for those we claim as kin.

Yes, there are failures of this kind of love. But even with those failures, we know deep in our bones—in our genes, memories, even our souls—that we're meant to care for our own. That we're connected. That we're not meant to go it alone. Because we are *one family*.

Sophia means wisdom, that key form of intelligence that applies experience and insight to challenges and opportunities that arise. Wisdom isn't just knowledge—it's what we do with it. It remembers what hurt us and doesn't repeat it. It remembers what helped or healed, and works to preserve and share it. Wisdom plants in good soil, because it has learned the consequences of planting in sand. It prepares for tomorrow by remembering yesterday.

Wisdom is reflection, yes—but also decision. Application. Learning that sticks. Learning that acts. So when I say *philosophia*, I don't mean elitist theories. I mean something essential to human flourishing: the "love of wisdom." The desire to seek it, hold onto it, nurture it and grow it. Philosophy, in its truest sense, is not a game. It's a guide. We should love and nurture wisdom. It is often in short supply. A true philosopher isn't someone debating abstractions for fun. It's someone who *loves wisdom* enough to pursue, preserve and foster it. To live by it. To spread it. *We should all strive to be true philosophers.*

THE WISDOM OF LOVING

There's another way to read *philosophia*: the *wisdom of loving*. This flips the lens. Rather than valuing wisdom because it leads us to care, we value care because it is the wisest way forward. It's not just moral. It's smart. It works.

This idea shows up everywhere. Not just in Greek texts, but in every culture: a hunger for wise, mutual care. Here the insights from experience reveal how best to bring peace and well-being to every one of our lives: *mutual care*. Treating others as we wish to be treated.

This means simply that *we all contribute* to our mutual well-being as we're able, and *we all receive* the essentials we need: food, clothing, housing, healthcare, education and safety. We choose to see these not as rare commodities that must be fought over—with some not getting what they need because someone else grabbed and hoarded it—but as real and genuine abundance that is gladly and wisely shared with everyone, without exception.

Everyone gives what they can. Everyone gets what they need. This isn't hard. It isn't naïve. It isn't utopian. It's wise. It's sustainable.

It's how we survive—and thrive. It's wisdom. The *wisdom* of *loving each other*.

Yes, some will take advantage. Some always have. But there are also always those who give more than they take. Who step up. Who sacrifice. Who hold the system together.

And the solution to bad actors—whether bullies or freeloaders—is not to build a society on hoarding and fear. The answer is not to glorify predators, or design systems to reward those who push others down.

The answer is to build systems around mutual care—and resist those who threaten it.

Our norm must be mutual care, not the combat of thieves.

In a culture of mutual care, all your needs are met. So are your family's. And your neighbors'. And your descendants'. And everyone else's. And when they are strong, you are stronger too. There's no hoarding. No exploiting. Just a shared commitment to each other's thriving. That's *philo-sophia*. The *wisdom* of *loving*.

THE GOLDEN RULE

What follows is a brief survey of what's often called the "Golden Rule"—the shining wisdom of mutual care across faiths, philosophies and worldviews. The count in parentheses is the estimated number of current followers, whether actively practicing or not, if known. These numbers aren't meant to suggest one tradition is more important than another, but simply to show how many people across the world identify with views that contain one shared insight: a golden rule of caring for others as we each should be cared for. (For an extended look, see *The Golden Rule* in **Sources**.)

Bahá'í Faith (~5 million)
"Lay not on any soul a load that you would not wish to be laid upon you, and desire not for anyone the things you would not desire for yourself." (Bahá'u'lláh, *Gleanings From the Writings of Bahá'u'lláh*)

Buddhism (~500 million)
"Treat not others in ways that you yourself would find hurtful." (*Udānavarga* 5.18 – 6th century B.C.E.)

Christianity (~2.5 billion)
"So in everything, do to others what you would have them do to you, for this sums up the Law and the Prophets." (Jesus, Matthew 7:12, *The Bible*)

Confucianism (~7 million)
"One word which sums up the basis of all good conduct…loving kindness. Do not do to others what you do not want done to yourself." (Confucius, *Analects* 15.23)

Hinduism (~1.2 billion)
"This is the sum of duty; do not do to others what would cause pain if done to you." (*Mahābhārata* 5, 1517)

Humanism, Atheism and Agnosticism (number unknown)
"Humanists try to embrace the moral principle known as the 'Golden Rule', otherwise known as the ethic of reciprocity, which means we believe that people should aim to treat each other as they would like to be treated themselves – with tolerance, consideration and compassion." (Maria MacLachlan, *Think Humanism*, 10/2007)

Islam (~1.9 billion)
"Not one of you truly believes until you wish for others what you wish for yourself." (*Hadith* 13, *40 Hadith an-Nawawi*)

Jainism (~4.2 million)
"One should treat all creatures in the world as one would like to be treated." (*Sūtrakṛtāṅga* 1.11.33)

Judaism (~15.3 million)
"You shall love your neighbor as yourself: I am the Lord." (Leviticus 19:18b, *Tanakh*)
"What is hateful to you, do not do to your neighbor. This is the whole of the Torah; all the rest is commentary. Go study." (Hillel, *Talmud*, *Shabbat* 31a)

Native American Spirituality (number unknown)
"We are as much alive as we keep the earth alive." (Chief Dan George)
"All things are our relatives; what we do to everything, we do to ourselves. All is really One." (Black Elk)

Sikhism (~26 million)
"I am a stranger to no one; and no one is a stranger to me. Indeed, I am a friend to all." (*Guru Granth Sahib*)

Taoism (~9 million)
"Regard your neighbor's gain as your own gain, and your neighbor's loss as your own loss." (Laozi, *T'ai-Shang Kan-Ying P'ien*)

Unitarianism (number unknown)
"We affirm and promote respect for the interdependent web of all existence of which we are a part." (Unitarian Universalist Association)

Yoruba (Nigeria) (~8.8 million)
"One going to take a pointed stick to pinch a baby bird should first try it on himself to feel how it hurts." (Yoruba proverb)

Zoroastrianism (~200,000)
"Do not do unto others whatever is injurious to yourself." (*Shāyast ne-Shāyast*)

These teachings are not limited to religion. Many early philosophers—writing centuries before modern religious structures—also expressed principles of mutual care.

Ancient Philosophers

Thales (c. 624–546 B.C.E.)
"Avoid doing what you would blame others for doing."

Sextus the Pythagorean (date uncertain)
"What you do not want to happen to you, do not do it yourself either."

Plato (c. 428–347 B.C.E.)
"Ideally, no one should touch my property or tamper with it, unless I have given him some sort of permission, and, if I am sensible, I shall treat the property of others with the same respect."

Isocrates (436–338 B.C.E.)
"Do not do to others that which angers you when they do it to you."

Epicurus (341–270 B.C.E.)
"It is impossible to live a pleasant life without living wisely and well and justly, and it is impossible to live wisely and well and justly without living pleasantly." (Note: "Justly" refers to reciprocal agreements against inflicting or suffering harm.)

Seneca the Younger (c. 4 B.C.E.–65 C.E.)
"Treat your inferior as you would wish your superior to treat you." (*Letters*, 47)

Aristippus of Cyrene (d. 365 B.C.E.)
"Cherish reciprocal benevolence, which will make you as anxious for another's welfare as your own."

A RECIPROCAL CALL TO ACTION

One common interpretation of these many examples of the Golden Rule, "Do unto others as you would have them do unto you," is the idea that these are mostly passive—about restraint rather than action—a version of *live and let live*, or *coexist*.

Appealing and valuable as that is, it is not the Golden Rule. In virtually every context in which the rule is found and expounded, it is about *taking action*, not refraining from it. We don't all get our needs met when we ignore the needs of others.

Do unto others is a command to *do something*—the very same thing you yourself would need, and that others should also be *doing for you*.

That's the *Golden Rule*, and it is the *true wealth* mined from each other's gifts to meet each other's needs. It is far more valuable than any shiny metal mined from the earth.

The Golden Rule is *a reciprocal call to action*. To *mutual* care. It is also found in the foundations of all just legal systems, in our own day and in history. More on this in an upcoming chapter.

THE GOLD IN THE GRAVEL

The examples above aren't meant to be exhaustive but illustrative. The original texts offer more nuance and depth, and a deeper dive is available in *The Golden Rule* in **Sources**.

Of course, there are stories, teachings and rules in many of the original texts that would seem to flatly contradict what we see above. Beyond that, there are countless bullies who have misused the religions and traditions of their subjects to manipulate and coerce them into horrific acts.

I contend that we can justly reject the contradictions and bad acts. We have no obligation to embrace them simply because they litter our common history. We need to discern the gold in the gravel, pick it out, and leave the gravel behind.

And this, too: That moment in the third-floor apartment—seeing that mom and her three kids—changed me. At the time, I'd never traveled farther than Canada. Since then, I've visited countries and cultures all over the world.

They dress differently. They have many different things they say or do to remind themselves of what they believe and their family histories: beads, books, ankhs, scrolls, crosses, stars, foods, tablets, totems, amulets, stained glass, languages, songs, chants, poems, myths, stories, herbs, stuffed toys, paintings, calendars, notebooks, icons, dances, statues, crescents, photographs, robes, special garments, ties, tattoos, tassels, incense, symbols, head coverings, and so much more. I take no issue with any of it. I have my own little reminders—tokens of meaning. We all do.

I've now met thousands of people of every shape, size and color. I've stayed in the homes and with the families of many people of many faiths and none.

With only rare exceptions, they were warm, welcoming and kind. They loved each other. They cared for each other. They cared for me when I was with them. I cared for them. My eyes were opened:

We are *one* family, and it is only *our mutual care* that can save us all.

It is the secret of the ages. And our future.

MOTHER OF EXILES

If we are to free each other from slavery, in all its forms and disguises, we must be clear-eyed about our own vulnerabilities. Bullies and parasites rely on them to keep us in our place—especially our *fear of the other*, our instinctive reactions to the unfamiliar, and even our misreading of things we don't fully understand or perceive.

"That Black Man"

I'm certain that fear was the root of the hot and angry objections to "that black man" coming to our all-white church in our all-white suburb. I'd never heard anyone there overtly identify as a racist or white supremacist, and I suspect they would have been horrified had they been accused of such things. But the fear was there, and it erupted the moment their protected perimeter was approached by someone *other*.

Though I was early on taught to value and respect others, I suspect racism had taken quiet root in me too—not as overt hatred, but as some implicit, subtle fear or miscomprehension of people who didn't look or act like me. It took time and a lot of travel to kill those bitter roots and teach me to value, respect and actually *enjoy* the enormous diversity of humanity.

But when we finally *get it*, we're much harder to fool or manipulate.

Turning Their Enemies Into Your Enemies

Friends might prank each other with fake snakes or spiders—harmless scares that prompt a laugh once the truth is seen. But bullies and parasites do something darker. They manufacture fear by inventing enemies—caricaturing people as monsters, threats or villains.

They demonize others to try to turn *them* into *your* enemies, claiming *those people* are conditioned to do evil and must be dealt with ruthlessly. And when they do that, and there are deaths of any others nearby? Dismissed as collateral damage.

Or they speak of *them* as Aristotle did—as a lower class of beings. We are their *betters*, they claim. The rest are fit only to serve the high-born above them, or to be sacrificed as needed.

Or they confine *them* to the ghettos, branding *them* as lazy, dirty, dangerous—then red-lining their neighborhoods and nations, locking them in place *by law* so they can't move or work.

Or they stoke fear of *them* if the "others" are *immigrants*—branding *them* as criminals, rapists, the diseased, the insane—to keep *them* away. It's the same smear, recycled across *every* wave of immigrants—Irish, Italians, Poles, Jews, Germans, Mexicans, Arabs, Asians, Muslims, Catholics, Hispanics... and, and, and.

Even the people who were here already—Native Americans—weren't spared. They were branded as "savages," forcefully removed by the army from the land they'd occupied for centuries, and killed if they resisted.

This isn't some imagined, revisionist, "liberal guilt" fiction. It's real history, and we need to acknowledge it—or we will repeat the worst atrocities of our past.

IMMIGRANTS

Fear of the other is a time-tested way to convince us that immigrants will *steal* our resources rather than help *increase* them. But every wave of immigrants has ultimately benefited us, rising from demonization to respect—because they were *productive*. They *added* to our resources. (The obvious exception, of course, is when the "immigrants" were armed colonizers who enslaved the people already here.)

We've seen these tactics used to fool and manipulate us—stoking fear, dread and revulsion instead of respect or sympathy. Time and again, we've demonized entire populations for the actions of a few bullies and parasites among them. *Our* bullies and parasites magnified—or invented—theirs to make us fear *all* of them. But most were just ordinary people, *like us*, like *you*, trying to be safe and productive, in a country that stands as a beacon of freedom, and whose founding documents declare *human rights* unalienable—for all *humans*, not just "citizens." (See the upcoming chapter *Our Rights and Obligations* for more.)

Let's pause for a moment and recall who we are. When France honored the vision and virtue of the United States with the gift of the Statue of Liberty, it required our building a massive foundation on which to stand. This sonnet, now displayed proudly within, was written by poet Emma Lazarus to help raise the funds for that foundation.

Lazarus titled the sonnet "The New Colossus" to contrast it with the Colossus at Rhodes, which celebrated a military victory. Note how clearly the differences in meaning are set forth, and especially the name given this mighty woman, declaring her *character* and *caring* to all the suffering peoples of the world: **Mother of Exiles**!

Mother of Exiles

Not like the brazen giant of Greek fame,
With conquering limbs astride from land to land;
Here at our sea-washed, sunset gates shall stand
A mighty woman with a torch, whose flame
Is the imprisoned lightning, and her name
Mother of Exiles. From her beacon-hand
Glows world-wide welcome; her mild eyes command
The air-bridged harbor that twin cities frame.

"Keep, ancient lands, your storied pomp!" cries she
With silent lips. "Give me your tired, your poor,
Your huddled masses yearning to breathe free,
The wretched refuse of your teeming shore.
Send these, the homeless, tempest-tost to me,
I lift my lamp beside the golden door!"

Emma Lazarus, 1883
for the Statue of Liberty

Let's all stop, set aside the hot political rhetoric of our current moment, and try hard to remember *who we are*, and where *we* came from.

Our own families came through that golden door, many of them tired, poor, "wretched refuse," homeless, huddled masses, tempest-tost, yearning to breathe free. And now that *we are safe*, taken in by the Mother of Exiles, we dare to refuse just the same welcome to those who follow after us?

Really? Is that who we have become? Are we now the angry neighbor that yells, "Get out of my yard!" at the family who fled their storm wrecked home or who escaped abuse and threat of death?

Mother of Exiles, open our eyes.

ILLEGAL ALIENS

"But they broke the law!" That may be technically true—just as those who drank from segregated water fountains broke the law, or those who sheltered Jews in Nazi Germany did. But legality is not the same as morality. Using the word "illegal" to redefine someone's worth, to defame them and justify rejecting their humanity, is a *tactic* as old as fear itself. It doesn't clarify the situation. It manipulates it.

When we declare something "illegal"—like a Black man drinking from a "whites-only" fountain—we take an act that's neither immoral nor dangerous and declare it against "the law." Now, conveniently, that person is a *lawbreaker*, a criminal. And once they're a *criminal*, we justify what follows: beating, jail, lynching... or deportation without due process: without rights, justice or fair hearing.

And let's be clear: "Illegal alien" is a double smear.

When we call someone "alien," we cast them as "other." *Not one of us.* Not *our* family. Not our responsibility. We act not like a nation founded by refugees, but like a classic mob—boss at the top, crew chiefs below, protection rackets, exploitations, bribes, enforcers: defending our own and shutting out anyone else. That becomes our morality: loyalty to the boss and the family, and disregard for anyone outside it.

Though immigrants have done nothing despicable or immoral—only fled cruelty, oppression and poverty, in search of safety and a future—we instead have *defined* them as *alien*. And we *alienate them from the very rights* that we ourselves claim are "*unalienable*" in our Declaration of Independence.

We claim that all people are created equal, with unalienable rights to life, liberty and the pursuit of happiness—rights "endowed by our Creator." These rights are *not* granted by *citizenship* but by *our shared humanity*. From our country's founding, we asserted that no king, president, government or law could take these rights away from *anyone*. It is a moral betrayal—utter hypocrisy—to pretend these rights apply only to those we approve of, and deny them to those we don't.

This is not just a matter of legality—it's a moral and rhetorical shell game. *Yes*, entering without authorization violates current immigration law. But using that fact alone to paint *all* undocumented immigrants as criminals is *misdirection*—a reframing designed to short-circuit our natural empathy and reinforce fear.

This tactic lets political actors collapse vastly different people and situations into a single, threatening image: asylum seekers, visa overstays, undocumented laborers and the like, are lumped together with thieves and violent criminals into one "alien menace."

And once this tactic is normalized, it's dangerously easy to expand its logic: "They're here illegally, therefore criminal." And if any of them dare disagree with any politician's actions—a right guaranteed to absolutely everyone in the First Amendment—then they are arrested, jailed, deported, or worse. And with no fair hearing, evidence, trial and judgement—rights guaranteed to absolutely everyone, not just citizens, in the Fifth and Fourteenth Amendments? Really?

And that's how nations have gone from "immigration enforcement" to ethnic cleansing. And how invaders have driven out, "relocated" or murdered the innocent inhabitants of the territories they coveted.

We are not the angry neighbor. We are the Mother of Exiles. We have to remember who we are.

The right question to ask about *any* immigrants isn't "Why do *I* have to take care of *them*?"

It must be, "How would *I* want to be received if *I* were fleeing cruelty, oppression and poverty?"

What would *I* want and need? Decide what the answer is—then *do that*.

Let's claim this insight. It makes us harder to manipulate—with propaganda, false narratives, manufactured enemies and fake heroes. It's time for that to end.

Our question must never be, "How can we get that poor, wretched refuse, those huddled masses *yearning to breathe free*, out of our yard and out of our sight?"

Treating others the way *we* want to be treated, our first question must always be, "How can we help?"

The solution?

Don't start with fear. Start with *mutual care*, instead. It always brings thriving and abundance.

And *strategize* it. Figure it out. Invest in caring, training, integration into our norms and culture, into who we are. It will always prosper us.

We can do this.

(Find an extended look at *Fear of the Other* and *Helping Immigrants and Homeless*, in **Sources**.)

JOINING RIGHTS AND OBLIGATIONS

When we fully recognize the thefts, lies and villainy of bullies and parasites, we must resist and restrain them. And if we've in any way served their ends—through silence, complicity, or imitation—we must stop, awaken, and stand with those who care.

To accomplish this, we must fully recognize, specify, implement and defend the rights *and obligations* of those who were once victims—once enslaved, once forced to subsidize the few. In other words: *us*.

We *who were taken from*—robbed of our time, labor and worth—must become more than just survivors. We must *unite*: an accepted, willfully *embraced* family with a shared union, a beloved community, building a society whose *core value* is mutual care rather than mortal combat.

Communism? Fascism? Socialism? Eugenics? Fantasy? Madness? Cults? Utopia? It isn't hard to list failed efforts that purported to free the enslaved and build an equitable and just society. They are abundant.

But the list of societies built for the few at the expense of many is far longer. Hundreds of millions have suffered and died for the pleasure of a few—far more than from efforts to build fairness for all.

Both have failed. But like seeds in spring, those that land in fertile soil—mutual care—will grow and thrive.

Former slaves—those who grasp the genius and necessity of mutual care—are finally the tillers of fertile soil. They plant, tend and grow the future of humanity. Former slaves, who now work for each other, are the parents of children born in freedom.

The enslaved have always been the source of abundance. Their hands built the world the bullies claim as their own creation. The slaves' daily genius and willingness have created all the technology, medicine, science, justice and wealth that exist, though much of it is exploited and hoarded by their "masters"—who also claim credit.

As these masters are replaced by those who are free, the measures of success are also replaced: The champions are not those who beat and defeat others and strive for power, or who enslave and rob us, but rather those who best embody, foster and defend mutual care.

But mutual care does not advance with mere hoping or slogans. There must be a clear understanding of what qualifies and what fails, what must be protected and what must be expended—to make it substantive, real and lasting.

The loving wisdom of the ancient and contemporary luminaries, the seers and teachers, provides the vision and sets the standard for why and how we are to care for each other. They give us a clear goal: mutual care. But to reach it, we need an equally solid foundation of rights and obligations. One cannot succeed without the other.

FOR EACH, FROM EACH

Mutual care produces abundance, not deprivation. Of course.

When we focus only on our *rights*, then *taking what's ours* seems like a solution to inequity. But it isn't. Taking is what bullies do. Taking ensures conflict. We need to think this through more fully.

When we awaken to true mutual care, our *obligation* to mutual *giving* is the solution, and cultivates peace. Rights and obligations are yoked.

Put plainly: Unalienable rights come with unavoidable obligations. True freedom isn't a lack of responsibility—it's freedom through shared responsibility. When we selfishly hoard and protect only what's "ours," we guarantee conflict and collapse.

Think of it this way. We live together as a beloved community: one big family, in one big house. We have shared spaces and private rooms. When any of us is sick, unless we help them to get better, we can all get sick. Infections happen and spread, and only by caring for the one of us who gets an infection do we best protect all of us from getting ill.

If there is a fire in one room, I don't let it burn if it isn't my room. That would be uncaring, but also stupid. I help put it out because it is right, and smart. And of course I help clean up the mess and fix any damage. It's what I'd want from others if it was my room that burned.

And our children (natural and adopted), as they grow, *all* need to learn to do the laundry, and cook, and clean up, and work, and fix the toilet when it clogs—or know to ask for help if it's beyond their skills. We teach them these things so they can *thrive* and *contribute* well to *our common life*.

Their *education* benefits them *and us*! Depriving them of education—because they come from a different room in the house, or because they can't afford it—is wrong, foolish and *deprives all of us*. It's that simple.

Any one of us can rightfully assert, "I have a right to an education!" or "I have a right to fire protection!" or "I have a right to healthcare!" But that can't work until each of us finally understands our obligation to help fulfill each of those rights for each other. That's the essence of *mutual* care, the wisdom of loving: Not only do we each receive what we need, *we each supply* what the others need.

Bullies and parasites make us all slaves for their benefit. They cause deprivation and poverty. They steal from us, hoard it, and keep us bound by lies, laws and fear.

Mutual care *frees us* from their control, and causes thriving and abundance. Truth, justice and joy become our common, simple norm.

TAXING OURSELVES

Here's how thriving happens in a modern, just and caring society: taxes.

Now before you scream and throw this book across the room, hear me out. This topic is so fraught with special privileges, fraud, theft, burdens, heavy-handed enforcement, unequal treatment and public distrust that any kind of genuine and useful purpose is difficult to even talk about in polite company. I get it.

So let's take a step back and think through how we go about mutual care for our one giant family: room by room and in common areas, in our one giant home.

The first and most obvious consideration is *common* areas. Some of our common needs can only be met by shared effort, and sometimes only over generations.

Our road system is a key example of this, and easily understood: We all benefit from well-built, safe roads, and the rules that govern their use, so they are sustained, and we are not put in danger by bad or inconsiderate drivers. Both the roads and the enforcement of rules of conduct on them are paid for by our taxes.

Of course, it is essential that all of this be done honestly. When bribery, corruption or special privileges occur, they are simply more examples of bullies and parasites stealing from the rest of us. We must not permit it.

But we all need the roads, and we all benefit from them, and so *we tax ourselves* to build and manage *together* what none of us could do alone. This is a simple example of *mutual care*. We can and should determine how best to share and spend the taxing of ourselves, but clearly a common effort is required for common needs.

Also note this vital truth: Common need does not mean simultaneous or identical. Rather, these are needs that we each have in common, though they may arise at different times and to different degrees.

Consider: Today I may spend my time at home, working on this book, in my pottery studio, in the yard checking on my tomatoes, or relaxing with my family—and never leave the house. No personal road use at all.

Tomorrow I'll go to work, run a few errands, visit a friend, go to the barber, and shop at the grocery store with my wife.

Next month I'll take a long drive to another city for a meeting and a brief vacation.

Several years ago, my wife and I were in a near-fatal car crash. An ambulance with paramedics came and took us to a hospital.

Last week the postal service delivered a box of three-ring paper and binders, which I'll use to print what you are now reading here, so I can do some layout evaluation and editing.

Every one of these examples involves the *common* use of roads, from no personal use on one day, to short and long drives by me personally, to transporting us by ambulance, to delivery of materials I use in my writing.

The common use of roads by all of us, for all the vital activities of our common life—shipping, transit systems, medical, shopping, work, visiting, relaxation—requires a *common sharing* to build and maintain this vital *common benefit*.

So it is also for our common defense: against fire, thieves and foreign aggressors. We pay in common through our taxes for what each and every one of us require, and that protects all of us.

If your house is on fire, I don't want it burning uncontrolled next to mine—and starting mine on fire—just because you couldn't afford to have your own fire-department protection. When I contribute to *common* fire protection, I help protect you and I *also* gain protection.

When I contribute to *common* roads, I give the fire department a way to get to your house or mine if there is a fire. You and I both help support all the shipping, transit, errands, work, travel, safety and more that *all of us* need.

It isn't much of a leap to see the wisdom and rightness of this when it comes to healthcare—yet no area of common need is more noisily contested or abused. We will explore it next.

MAKING HEALTHCARE MUTUAL

Were there none who were discontented with what they have, the world would never reach anything better. – Florence Nightingale

Imagine if only the wealthy were allowed on the roads. Or only full-time executives, or only those born in certain ZIP codes. That would be outrageous—unwise, unjust, foolish and immoral. But that's literally how we treat healthcare in the United States today. Florence Nightingale called out complacency. And our system rewards cruelty, preserves suffering, and withholds care from those who need it most.

In our current system, the wealthy and powerful are treated as worthy of health. Executives, supervisors and full-time employees are protected. But those below them—those who work part-time, or can't work at all—are often denied care or sent away with scraps. The implication is chilling: that their lives matter less. That their health is expendable. That the disabled and the poor are somehow less human.

Those who work too far below, as well as those who don't or can't work, are denied coverage, or given limited, marginal care, and sent away. Denying healthcare to the poor and disabled is more than neglect—it echoes eugenics, the belief that only some lives are worth preserving.

Healthcare in the United States today isn't just broken. It's hijacked. Yes, there are excellent caregivers and medical facilities. But the system and its mechanisms—insurance, billing, approval chains, payment gatekeepers—has profit motives so dominant, they routinely overrule medical judgment and deny care. And those who defend this sickening system do so because it *enriches* them. Money that *should* go to treatment is siphoned off into company profits and stockholder dividends.

Those profits don't come from innovation. They come from denial. By slashing care, delaying treatment and burying patients in red tape, insurers reduce expenses—and call that savings. Denial of care is literal *theft* from those who need care. It is *skimming*, corporate *stealing* protected by jargon, lies, propaganda and lobbyists. (Remember the cashier, the programmer, the bank, the energy company?) Look:

THE EVIDENCE OF THEFT

The executive pay figures below come straight from a major U.S. health-insurance company's own annual report. This isn't hearsay—these are *their* numbers. And they tell the story plainly. As is the norm for the claims in this book, it's available under *Healthcare* in **Sources**, along with others, with links to the original documents for each company.

The CEO receives $23.5 million per year. That's $1,958,333 per month, or $13,232 per hour. Plus full, top-tier healthcare coverage, of course.

The four executives who report directly to him make every year:
$16,100,000 or $1,341,667 per month. $9065 per hour.
$16,100,000 or $1,341,667 per month. $9065 per hour.
$10,200,000 or $850,000 per month. $5743 per hour.
$6,200,000 or $515,000 per month. $3491 per hour.

These four executives all get gold-plated, denial-free healthcare. No restrictions for any prescription, doctor, procedure or therapy—since they are in charge of those decisions. These salaries are made possible not by quality of care—but by denial of care to others. You and me.

At the same time, in the same country, a typical retail clerk makes $7.25 to $15 per hour, struggles to cover monthly rent for a room, and isn't covered for health insurance by the employer.

What does it say about a country where the people most essential to the system's functioning—retail workers, caregivers, laborers—are often the least protected by it?

The treatment of the most needy is despicable. But it isn't just those at the bottom of this unbalanced wage-and-benefit scale who struggle. Even "upper-middle-class" families with two incomes struggle—with rent, mortgages, insurance premiums, deductibles and co-pays—only to then face denials of coverage. And "appeals" processes are so utterly aggravating and lengthy that most don't bother to try to begin one.

Do we also realize that "co-pays" and "deductibles" are a part of this same for-profit scheme? Those clever labels make it all *seem* normal. That's just how the healthcare system works... Really?

We need to *see this* plainly: If you are *required to pay* a co-pay or deductible, it's only because they *didn't* pay it. Shifting expenses *onto you* increases their profits. Why are we paying these *extras*—when we *already pay* for coverage? If your house catches fire, does homeowners insurance require a co-pay to send the fire truck? Of course not.

Why are we forced to pay "co-pays" and "deductibles"? It's just another absurd trick—offloading *their* costs onto *us* to boost *their* profits.

We can't unsee this anymore. And we shouldn't try.

WHAT ABOUT UNIVERSAL HEALTHCARE?

For decades, the health-insurance industry has convinced legislators, and us, that universal healthcare—i.e., fair, equal coverage for everyone, paid for by everyone—is dangerous and unworkable—a "socialist nightmare," as if fairness itself were a threat. Meanwhile, countless other nations prove daily that it isn't.

And for decades, the poor and those with "pre-existing conditions" were excluded—barred from coverage altogether. Until…

Enter the Affordable Care Act of 2010—fiercely opposed by the insurance industry then, and still under attack now. The ACA uses public funds to help low-income people—who simply can't afford health insurance—to be able to afford to buy it, based on their income.

And it mandates coverage for "pre-existing" conditions. This was previously a clever "out" insurance companies gave themselves. If they could establish that you had a disease or injury prior to buying insurance from them, they'd refuse to cover anything related to it. Even worse, they'd refuse to allow individuals with certain conditions, such as autism, to purchase health insurance *at all*. If you were diagnosed with that (or dozens of other conditions), you were refused coverage entirely. You literally could not buy health insurance.

Many of those who benefit today from the coverage mandates of the ACA don't even realize they have coverage *because* of it, or that this law had to be passed simply to *get* coverage! That ignorance is itself a symptom of the propaganda and manipulation surrounding this topic.

So the Affordable Care Act provided coverage for those with incomes so low they previously couldn't afford to buy health insurance at all, plus a mandate to make sure *all* health needs are covered! That sounds practical and compassionate, and *it is*. It *helped*—but didn't change the core *theft* at the heart of the system—the use of *denial of care* to *create profits* for companies and executives. Some still suffer so others can prosper.

Here's why: The insurance plans offered under the ACA still run through the same insurance companies—companies that can and do deny care whenever it reduces their costs. Denial remains a tool to protect executive pay and profits.

Between the money *we pay* and the professionals *who care for us* stands a middleman parasite, misnamed as "insurance"—diverting funds and celebrating the diversion as profit. This is true of both private and employer insurance—and even of ACA plans. The money still flows through the same insurance companies. And part of it still skimmed off for the executives, and corporate profits.

We really should legislate equal healthcare for all—it's the right thing to do. But it's another thing altogether when our taxes support theft designed into the system—to profit executives (and shareholders) who game that system by denying care. These are people who preserve suffering so they can prosper. That's what parasites do.

Profit isn't inherently evil. But in healthcare, where literal life and death are on the line, profit as an incentive is both immoral and dangerous. When profit thrives on human suffering—on sickness untreated, medication withheld, procedures denied—it becomes a parasite feeding on our very lives.

Most advanced nations—and many less wealthy ones—already understand this. They treat healthcare as a human right, not a financial battleground. Their systems are overseen by competent professionals who are well-compensated, not absurdly enriched.

The difference? *They don't use people's suffering as a revenue stream.* The people who supervise healthcare systems there are appropriately compensated. It isn't *theft* in those countries and systems, and their national healthcare outcomes are *better than ours*—for infant mortality, life expectancy and cost per person. (Details in *Healthcare* in **Sources**.)

Also, consider what we pay our top leaders over healthcare in our *own* national government. They lead complex organizations with thousands upon thousands of employees.

The Surgeon General of the United States is paid $191,000 per year.
The head of Health and Human Services is paid $246,000.
The head of the Centers for Disease Control is paid $183,200.
Even the President of the United States is paid just $450,000.

We can obviously attract skilled, gifted, capable leaders without paying them $23,000,000 per year!

We're *fully capable* of building a universal healthcare system—coverage for everyone, paid for by everyone—managed competently at every level. Once we make that moral and intelligent decision, the rest is logistics. We know how to do it. We *can* make it work. But we must eliminate the incentives to profit that come from denying care.

How Does It Work in Other Countries?

In countries with universal healthcare, everyone receives care—equally. It's funded through common taxes for the common good. No bills for doctor visits, medications or surgery. Everyone gets what they need. Everyone contributes. It's *mutual care*.

Opponents in the U.S. tell horror stories—of patients waiting years for care—and try to scare us with terms like "socialized medicine" or "bureaucrats will dictate your healthcare decisions." Or some other sinister-sounding label meant to make us look away. But look closer:

Are we really to believe our current system is better? A nightmarish complicated contraption: A scheme where pharmaceutical companies can charge outrageous amounts for common drugs. Where insurance businesses *dictate treatment*, *deny coverage*, and base profits and bonuses on how much care they refuse. An endless labyrinth of coverages no one seems to understand, full of supplementary plans, teeth and eyes somehow not a part of your body and requiring separate coverage, endless forms to repeatedly complete, loopholes, exclusions, confusion and red tape—designed to enrich some by keeping others sick. **This** is the system we're supposed to defend or believe is **better**?

I don't think we're gullible enough to believe that anymore.

Scary Stories

What about the horror stories in other countries—long waits to see a doctor or get surgery? They happen, but they're rare. Most of those stories are exaggerated, recycled endlessly to scare us. Some are just made up, fictions, corporate propaganda meant to keep us trapped in our profitable nightmare. (And some, as my brother calls them, are just "stupid stories"—minor annoyances we retell for a laugh or a groan. We rarely repeat stories about when things work well. It's the dumb or frustrating moments that stick. We like to recall the annoying anomalies.)

I've received healthcare in many countries, and I have friends living all over the world. Where care is universally available, it's typically quick enough, effective and caring. Real doctors and health workers care for you. Then you go home. No bills, no forms, no "claims," no phone battles for approvals. Just good medical care. It works.

Are there flaws in universal healthcare? Of course—every system has them. But they are the exception, not the rule. And even if others struggle, that doesn't mean we can't do better. We *should*. And we *can*.

The Logistics of Healthcare

Let's consider the logistics needed to create a system of universal healthcare, without a parasitic middleman layer. Is it beyond our abilities?

No. We build extensive roads and complex transit systems. We have air-traffic control and thousands of airplanes in the sky every minute of every day. We have humans on an international space station. We've sent probes to other planets, even out of our solar system. We coordinate global supply-chains across nations and oceans.

If we can manage space stations and overnight delivery, surely we can manage healthcare. *We have the know-how. What we've lacked—until now—is the will.*

The *logistics*, the organizational technology and delivery expertise we humans have evolved and developed is extraordinary. I once ran the division of a major software vendor that built such systems. I know firsthand that it *works*.

We can readily apply this logic to healthcare. Our health doesn't need to stay hostage to a mass of corporate parasites. We can center care on patients again.

We know how. We just have to choose to do it.

Does a mutual-care health system need good supervision, effective logistics, efficient delivery systems and individualized care from competent, well-trained medical professionals? Does it need quality control, regular updating and constant improvement?

Well, *of course*—just like any other large and complicated system does. *But we already know how to do this.* Look at our roads, our skies, our solar system, our stores and gas stations and electricity and natural-gas delivery, and the coffee pods that just arrived at your front door.

Again: *We know how to do this, and we can.*

Those who oppose it do so to protect their profits, not your health. They lie to scare you. They work with legislators to pass or defeat laws. All to protect their profits—not your health.

Our current profit-based system is like a cancerous mass that diverts life-giving blood from the rest of the body to itself. It pulses and grows while the patient withers away. A parasite, pure and simple.

It is past time to take our healthcare out of the wallets of bullies and parasites and create a just, compassionate system of mutual care—one rooted in justice, worthy of our humanity. We *tax ourselves* to do it. Of course. And it helps all of us to *thrive*.

Of course it must be done honestly, fairly, effectively. But it will be better—immediately better—than the nightmare we're in now. And there are excellent examples of this at work every day in other countries. We can emulate their best methods and organization.

We can do it well, maybe even better. We must, and we will.

Perhaps, Looking Back

The grotesque imbalances and over-compensations in our current healthcare system aren't listed here just to shock—they're here to help us think clearly and fearlessly about what's right and what's possible. The logic and imperative of mutual care must extend beyond healthcare, into every shared domain of our lives. We'll open these up in the pages ahead.

I hope that, someday in the future, readers of this book will look in disbelief at this section on healthcare: *Wait, the system used to let people suffer while others got rich off it? No way. That can't be real.*

I invite *your* insights and contributions into our common life, and how to make it better together. **MutualCare.online** is set up for just this purpose. We can share resources, ideas and courage for building a better world—together. Come aboard.

OUR RIGHTS AND OBLIGATIONS

Many humanist and religious philosophers have offered clear, illuminating insights into the wisdom of loving and mutual care. Even when some of their followers ignored or distorted their teachings, their wisest advocates still gave practical guidance for how to live it out. Mutual care naturally includes meeting our common *individual* needs—for food, clothing, housing, healthcare, education and safety.

Mutual care also includes needs *we share*: for roads, forests, rivers, oceans, natural resources and air. Those who destroy what we share don't just harm others. They sink the boat with all of us in it.

At its root, mutual care—meeting our individual and shared *needs*—is the *imperative joining* of rights and obligations: the *right* to receive and the *obligation* to give. Both must be understood more deeply if this is to work at all.

THE HISTORY OF RIGHTS

As clear as our rights may seem to us today, they were opaque to much of history. Genocidal tyrants took lives without care, and often with evil pleasure. Slavery was accepted as normal and exploitation as inevitable. Parasites stole the resources of entire continents to enrich and decorate another—at the expense of many "savage" lives.

No one had individual rights simply because they were born. Power and theft, bullies and parasites, determined who got what. You went along or you went away: to dig, to dungeon, or to death.

"Rights," when considered at all, were simply tools granted by rulers to preserve order. There were no intrinsic or unalienable rights—none based on your humanity. Even in ancient codes like Hammurabi's (~1800 B.C.E.), rights were privileges, *granted* by those in power—and just as easily revoked. Property, wives, children, even the right to kill—all could be taken at the whim of those who governed.

In 1493, Pope Alexander VI, invoking divine authority, decreed all land and *peoples* of the Western Hemisphere belonged to the rulers of Portugal and Spain:

> **Out of our own sole largess and certain knowledge and out of the fullness of our apostolic power, by the authority of Almighty God... we make, appoint,**

> and depute you and your said heirs and successors lords of them with full and free power, authority, and jurisdiction of every kind...

The indigenous people had *no* rights to their land—*or themselves*! It never crossed the minds of the European rulers. They were labeled "savages," enslaved, and sent to mine gold to adorn of the nobles of Europe. A horrified friar helped end the practice—only for the nobles to then replace it with the importation of African slaves.

Attempts to claim rights—or even just freedom from slavery—were always met with brutal punishment. Spartacus led a revolt and died for it; he and his followers were crucified and put on public display. Other rulers impaled their enemies and raised their corpses as warnings. Even today, modern cartels echo this savagery, making roadside exhibits of the mutilated bodies of tortured underlings who failed them.

Rights? Only when *granted*—by a ruler, for the ruler's own benefit.

Intrinsic Rights

It is only in recent centuries that the idea of *intrinsic* rights has gained any notable recognition or support. It is vital to know about this, because it set the stage for our current social and political realities, and it will be the foundation for a vastly better future.

Key Western proclamations of rights include three pivotal documents: the Magna Carta (England, 1215), the Declaration of the Rights of Man (France, 1789) and the Declaration of Independence (U.S., 1776).

The Magna Carta is often cited as an early model of individual rights—but in reality, it asserted the rights of powerful landowners (barons) to limit the king's whims, while preserving their own authority over serfs.

Rulers either claimed to be divine, or to rule by divine right—and acted by "force and will," with unchecked power. They had utter freedom to act, and they used imprisonment or murder to enforce their will and avoid all accountability. Some stirrings against this "divine right of kings" had begun in Europe, but with little result. Virtually everyone, even the most impoverished, were raised to believe the "divine right" fiction. Many still do today, all around the world. It disguises bullies with legitimacy, to their obvious benefit.

Individual Rights

The Magna Carta may have sparked a slow awakening to *individual* rights, but it didn't assert them. It was about powerful men asserting their power against a weak king they didn't especially fear. They stood up to him for *themselves*, not for "the universal rights of man." That wasn't even a glimmer in their minds.

I bear no animosity toward England's royal family or its public traditions, and I understand they're regarded as symbols of British pride and Empire, such as it is. But let's be clear: The divine right of kings still echoes in the monarch's title—"protector of the faith" of the Church of England—and the king still has sovereign immunity and lives off of the vast wealth seized long ago by the "force and will" of his predecessors and their conquests and theft.

Though royalty today is a faint shadow of its former power, it still symbolizes a deeper truth: For most of history, *slaves* and subjects have subsidized bullies and parasites. Wealth flows upward from the conquered to the conquerors. Monarchies across Europe and around the world still reflect this truth and live off its legacy. Their fortunes were not built by innovation or skill but by predation. Theft.

It is an unpleasant truth to see, but it *is* the truth. We must not forget it.

REPRESENTATIVE DEMOCRACY

It was against this reality that the movements for "representative democracy" began. Rather than rulers deciding what we must do, we imagined *choosing* leaders to carry out the will of the people—to *represent us*, leaders whose *motivation* was to *use their skills* for the *common* good. But we also retained the power to "unchoose" them if they failed at that task. We could vote them out of office.

This revolutionary idea was the demand for *rights for all*, well beyond the Magna Carta's narrow agreement between powerful land barons and a monarch.

Only two of the three documents noted earlier made a forceful claim about universal individual rights. At the time, "men" was broadly understood to mean "human beings"—though we know these rights were not equitably applied to women or to slaves.

Nevertheless, consider these short excerpts:

United States: "We hold these truths to be self-evident, that all men are created equal, that they are endowed by their Creator with certain unalienable Rights, that among these are Life, Liberty and the pursuit of Happiness. That to secure these rights, Governments are instituted among Men, deriving their just powers from the consent of the governed."

France: "1. Men are born and remain free and equal in respect of their rights; social distinctions can only be based on public utility. 2. The aim of every political association is the protection of the natural and imprescriptible rights of man; these rights are liberty, property, security and resistance to oppression."[1]

Each of these documents contains a revolutionary assertion: We have rights that *no one* can take away.

In France these rights are "*natural* and *imprescriptible*," literally meaning *in-born* and *unremovable*. The language reflects Enlightenment ideals—reason, liberty and human dignity as universal.

In the United States, these are *unalienable*—they can't be taken away—because humans are "*endowed* by their Creator." This was a late change to the language; earlier drafts resembled the French phrasing. But in a country founded by religious refugees, the text was reframed to reinforce a deeper truth: No human can take away what God has given as an *intrinsic* part of their creation.[2]

RIGHTS, WITH OBLIGATIONS

Here's where we must be thoughtful, intelligent and intentional:

As horrified as we are by the cruelty of bullies and parasites—who heartlessly, murderously used innocent lives to serve their own comfort—so too are we even more grateful for those before us and around us who stood up to defend human rights. We owe them thanks. We still need such people.

But here's the necessary insight for the future:

Our "unalienable" *rights* are preserved only when bound to *obligations* that are equal, imperative and permanent.

Rights *require* obligations. We protect *each other*.

I can't assert my rights without accepting my obligations to others.

---

[1] While both France and the U.S. made powerful declarations about rights, both were also deeply entangled in systems of inequality—enslavement, colonialism and disenfranchisement of women. This doesn't undermine the ideals but frames them more truthfully.
[2] And not ignoring the efforts by segregationists to define slaves as a different "order" of Creation, and thus *not endowed* with these rights. An ancient excuse.

A despot claims absolute rights, while imposing all obligations on his subjects. That's the failed model of the apex predator—everyone else serving his whims, fearing his wrath, surviving on crumbs.

MUTUAL CARE AND PROTECTION

We have rights and won't be *forced* to serve the *will* of bully kings. Instead, we join together to help each other thrive. We finally understand this: *Rights* are actually the recognition of universal, basic, human *needs*.

They can't be ignored at the will of someone in power. I have *rights* to stay alive, to be free, to pursue happiness, and to be secure in what is mine. Those reflect my most basic *needs* as a human being. Those needs, and the rights that protect them, are only met by *mutual obligation*.

When there is no monarch to "grant" rights (or not), and to protect them (or not), it is up to us to protect them for each other.

We protect and care for each other. I protect your rights; you protect mine. I meet your needs; you meet mine. That's *mutual* care. Neither of us can achieve the common good alone. Together we plant and protect the common soil and reap the abundance of our shared labor. We fulfill *each other's* needs and guard *each other's* rights.

That's the *Golden Rule*, and it is true wealth. It is far more valuable than the shiny metal mined from the earth.

That is the future of our rights: They are only preserved when we realize they are *fulfilled* by our obligations to each other.

If I want my rights protected, I must help protect yours. If I hope my needs will be met, I must be ready to help meet yours. Our rights and needs are fulfilled through each other's shared obligations and abilities. That's the wisdom—and imperative—of mutual care.

- Our *obligations*: to use our *abilities* for each other—to meet one another's needs and defend one another's rights.
- Our *rights*: to life, liberty, health, safety, and dignity—our most basic human needs, which no bully or parasite can justly deny.

In mutual care, our rights and obligations are yoked together.

In mutual care, *we rise* from exploitation in the fields, the factories, the prisons they built. *We rise* beyond conquest and cruelty. We leave the bullies and parasites—and slavery itself—to history.

In mutual care, *needs are met by shared abilities*—from each, for each—toward a future of peace and prosperity, thriving and abundance.

We replace exploitation with mutual care.

We will rise when we choose this way.

The Way of Mutual Care

How do we replace exploitation with mutual care? What are the *essentials* of this way of life? Here's a real-life example to start, a picture to help us think clearly about where our world is today, and what it needs to be whole and healthy…

We have always adopted animals, starting with a very old German Shepherd that had lived outside, largely neglected, on its elderly owner's front porch across the street from us.

When the owner died, no one came to claim or care for the dog, so we brought him home. The first night he howled and whimpered all night long, frightened and confused.

He was skinny, missing patches of hair, and had smelly sores on his back. We fed him, bathed him, petted and talked to him, and took him for long walks with our infant son. We loved him into the family.

It took time to build his trust, and for him to grasp that he was now safe, cared for and loved. The reality he had accepted as *normal*—fed, but otherwise neglected and stuck on a porch in all weather—was now gone.

The skin healed, the hair regrew, and he gained weight. For the few years he was with us, he was happy, content, caring and protective, especially of the little one, our infant son, whom he accompanied on our walks.

We've seen this same pattern with our subsequent adoptions of dogs that had clearly been abused. A newly adopted one once leapt from our car window and ran, so terrified as he was of *any* humans and the inevitable cruelty he expected from them.

It took about six weeks of constant care, and then one day he simply rolled over on his back for a belly rub, as if to say, "Safe at last." Like all the others, he became an integral, affectionate part of our family. It always takes time and persistence, but they all surrender to genuine care, and then they thrive and give love in return, mutual care, with willingness and joy.

Are there corrections needed in the course of caring? Sure—but *not* by cruelty. A dog quickly grasps that being accepted and loved in a family is worth the moments of correction. That's how they learn the ways of love. Anyone who's adopted or raised animals has seen this process at work.

The cynic in us says, *Yeah, well good luck with humans.* So let's just grant that humans are complicated, and often difficult, and some of them have grown up to become bullies and parasites. But now that we know we don't need them in charge, that we don't need to "stay in our place," we can see the way forward, take hold of the future, and change it. And we will.

Here are the *essentials* needed to reach this goal:

- A clear-eyed acceptance of how we've been kept in our place—our labor and lives enslaved and exploited for others' benefit, out of all proportion to our shared value as human beings.
- A rigorous understanding of propaganda and how to recognize it, starting in childhood. If we can teach kids not to accept candy from strangers, we can teach them not to fall for the lies of manipulation. But we must teach it—intentionally.
- The intentional and constantly reinforced teaching of *empathy*—being able to understand the nature, needs and fears of others. This does not mean a mindless acceptance of every difference as equally valuable, but it does mean seeking to consciously understand each other, to imagine oneself in their place, and ask, "How would I want to be treated, if that was me?"
- An insistence on rewarding growing skill and effort fairly—but not at the cost of subsidizing hoarding or privilege. Work should receive proportionate, just reward.
- An insistence on our *personal obligation to provide mutual care to everyone—no exceptions*. This includes food, clothing, housing, healthcare, education and safety—the essentials that make us healthy, capable contributors to the common good.
- Changing *ourselves*—our *families* and *neighborhoods*—first. We can't change the whole world at once, but we can change where we are. And that change will spread. *Think globally. Act locally.*
- Training, in families and schools, that teaches that mutual care as the highest good—the path to thriving and abundance. And honoring those who live it. Write it. Teach it. Insist on it.
- An awareness that bullies and parasites hijack even our best ideals—including mutual care—to seize power and drain our life and efforts. This was the fatal flaw in every failed utopia: socialism, communism, cults and more. Expose them.
- A readiness to swiftly stop those who try to gain power by harming or imposing control over others, or through threat, exploitation or fraud. Keep them from keeping us in our place. Resist and restrain.

Of course, there will be voices that belittle these necessary advances, will chuckle at our naïveté, rail about all the failed utopians over the course of history, and claim that—like it or not—only the reigning powers-that-be who stride above us now, and ruled throughout history, have the strength and right to run the world. And who sell us the lie that we are richer, more prosperous and healthy, than we'd be without them.

But it is all myth and lies, trickle-down nonsense. We must say *no* to bullies and parasites, and *yes* to mutual care. Then nothing will "trickle," and abundance can flow. We will thrive best without them.

ABUNDANCE AND LIBERTY

The most radical thing we can do with abundance is share it.

We live on a planet with such extraordinary abundance that we can easily provide every person with healthcare, decent housing, and good food. Anything short of this is evil.

Instead, the poor subsidize the rich. The slaves subsidize the lifestyle of the masters. Employees ensure the safety of their employers by giving up their own. The serfs toil, and the gentry enjoy the fruits of that labor. Soldiers march, slog, fight, suffer and die, and the nobles are kept secure. This is the constant pattern of history, and *the story of the world today*. It is time—long overdue—to change the plot.

As long as we cling to the fiction that evolution favors the "apex predator"—the strongest bully—then we'll accept *inequality* as natural, and resign ourselves to it, even approve of it.

In their vision, the social order is a fight—winners and losers. We celebrate those who claw to the top, leaving others wounded and discarded. The many apologists for this flawed vision are **dead wrong**.

Instead, if we embrace the value of *mutual care*—me for you, you for me—ensuring *each other's* food, clothing, housing, healthcare, education and safety, just as we'd protect our own children, then the same bright light would shine on all of us. None would be left in the foul darkness.

Every form and degree of slavery—coercion of some for the benefit of others—can come to an end. *It must.*

We all fund the fire department. They come wherever and whenever there's a fire—with equal urgency, rich or poor. We're smart enough to have figured this out for our shared safety. So how can we not be smart enough to realize the principle applies fully and rightly to each other's health? Or housing? Or food? Or education? Or safety?

Beyond these basics of mutual care, we should allow wide freedom in how people spend their time and income. Yes, all should contribute as able—and we wisely *tax ourselves* to ensure it. That's a norm we should teach early. But once our shared needs are met, we should celebrate the diversity of personal goals and interests.

Mutual care doesn't require conformity—of lifestyle, belief or expression. It's not control. It's just… mutual care.

- Care according to need. Everyone receives what they need—because everyone has rights.
- Contribute to the common good. Our shared obligations meet our shared needs.
- Celebrate joy and fulfillment. Be grateful—for each other and for life.

That's the ***real*** "survival of the fittest": Those who ensure the well-being of all. It truly is this simple.

The fittest best ensure well-being for themselves and their descendants. When all families act as one family, everyone prospers—not through hoarding, but through shared protection and care.

Those who take and hoard what others need are not fit. Their predatory actions should be condemned— never tolerated, much less celebrated.

Once again: ***In a lifeboat large enough for everyone, throwing others overboard and hoarding provisions does not prove your worthiness to be captain. It shows you should be in restraints.***

Stealing is not proof of superiority. Bullies and parasites are not heroes. Their self-praise is a lie. They *create* poverty and conflict. Never admire them.

This is a rich, abundant planet. Sharing the abundance makes us all rich—and free. It is the wisest way forward.

It will require a solid understanding of true leadership—not the seeking of power and wealth, but the wise and skilled supervising of cooperative action, with expertise and care.

Let's examine what this requires, starting with *authority*.

AUTHORITY – WHO IS IN CHARGE?

I suspect most of us don't give authority much thought—until it fails us. We tend to assume those in charge will do the right thing, and we only notice when they don't. Some of us seek positions of authority, some claim them without consent, some threaten or beat others into obedience, and still others would just as soon focus on other things. I for one would rather be working with clay in my studio, or taking a walk with my wife.

But, authority.

If we are to free ourselves from bullies and parasites and no longer be slaves, we had *damn well* better understand *authority*—and *fast*. Anarchists and poets have both said, "resist authority," but not much thought has gone into *what happens after the current authority is gone*—chaos? heaven on earth? limitless indulgence? … Or something worse?

All these potential futures, and a thousand others, have been imagined by the threat—or promise—of authority overturned. They all reveal how little we understand authority—and how deeply we disagree about what it even is. Let's invest some serious time and thought. It will teach us when and *who* to resist and restrain.

Otherwise, we will concede and accept a predatory hierarchy as inevitable.

FORMS OF AUTHORITY

There are many ways we experience authority in life. To better understand how it shapes us, for good or ill, it helps to distinguish four major forms:
- Acknowledged and respected – based on expertise
- Imposed, persistent and ingrained – enforced or inherited control
- Overthrown and replaced – through revolution or rejection
- Granted (consented or accepted) – such as elected leadership, employment oversight or project and safety supervision.

This last one is directly connected to true democracy and mutual care.

As these are each sketched in, it will be apparent that there are many areas of overlap and conflict, but understanding the key characteristics of each will open insights into our current inequities and miseries, and help us to find our way forward. Understanding which form we're under also helps us recognize when to resist—and when to build something better.

Acknowledged – What the Expert Knows or Believes

When we think of authority, we imagine someone making decisions and giving orders. But another vital form—often overlooked—is expertise: deep knowledge that informs those decisions. For supervising authority to function well, it must be paired with this kind of expertise.

In its best form, expertise means someone—or something—we can reasonably rely on for accurate knowledge or guidance. This includes people, institutions, libraries, digital databases or even artificial intelligence, when rightly used. And we should confess, all of us, that we often mistake confidence for expertise, an ancient problem only made worse by a worldwide internet, and both ignorant and malicious actors. We all tend to repeat assertions that confirm our opinions, even if we don't know if they're true. Let's do better. So, to expertise…

Two obvious areas of expertise are of significant benefit:
- an unfamiliar area of knowledge or skill, and
- detecting lies, fraud or other crimes.

An Unfamiliar Area of Knowledge or Skill

My brother is an expert cabinet-maker, with deep knowledge of wood, grains, saws, joining, sanding, glues, polishes, form, function and beauty. To someone unfamiliar with these things, he'd be an *authority* to study under, or to consult when making or evaluating furniture.

There are experts in every field—science, logistics, engineering, farming, transportation, medicine, nutrition, electronics, culture and more. The areas where there is or can be expert authority is vast and daunting, but their value is clear: When we need understanding, advice or solutions, we turn to those with proven knowledge and experience.

This is pretty simple: Seek an *authority* when expert knowledge and experience are needed.

Yes, there are complications—opinions confidently masquerading as expertise, or competing conclusions from different experts—but that doesn't invalidate the value of real expertise. There are people and institutions with deep knowledge and experience, and their *authority* on a topic can be very valuable. Deep knowledge, earned over time, is still one of our greatest tools for learning, action and progress. We can seek and gain from this, while acknowledging wariness of presumed experts who have proven to be frauds, or simply wrong. Let's think it through.

Detecting Lies, Fraud or Other Crimes

Expertise doesn't just help us build things—it helps uncover deception. Years ago, I was called as an expert witness in a lawsuit by a computer manufacturer suing a former employee and his new company, which was making and selling a competing product. The previous company alleged he stole their processor design and so his new income was based on theft.

I obtained the processor board of a computer from both companies. To the unaided eye—including the judge's—they looked quite different. The components varied in size, shape and layout. A non-expert would not find the claims of theft compelling.

But I ignored the surface differences and traced the entire circuitry of both boards, identifying the location and value of every resistor, capacitor, diode, transistor, integrated circuit, coil and transformer. The diagrams proved the underlying design was identical. I said so in deposition, and both legal teams immediately recognized the truth: The second company *had* stolen the design. They simply tried to disguise it.

This is the point: I was brought in as an *authority* by attorneys and a court which *did not have expertise on the subject*. I had no stake in the outcome—only knowledge. That's what real expert authority offers: clarity in confusion, resolution without *bias*.

The second company was plainly guilty of a theft they tried to disguise and deny—virtually the definition of a *parasite*. They were *resisted* by the creator of the design and ultimately *restrained* by the judge.

Detectives and forensic scientists use similar skills to solve crimes. So do language experts (uncovering forgeries or plagiarism), art historians, archaeologists and medical researchers and epidemiologists—exposing fake cures, faux crises and hoaxes meant to defraud the unwary.

Expertise in a field is crucial—not just for civilization's success, but for mutual care itself. Bullies and parasites know this, but they'll deny it. They attack real experts because knowledge threatens their power. We must guard true expertise fiercely—rejecting the fakes that bullies install, and defending the legitimacy of real, objective sources and fact-checkers.

We must learn to discern true expertise, which serves only truth, from the modern trend of paid and pseudo-experts—which have led to a growing distrust of legitimate experts in science, medicine, history and more—a distrust often deliberately stoked by bad actors. That's why educated, thoughtful, thorough *discernment* matters so much.

Real expert authority offers clarity in confusion, and resolution without *bias*. For more on this topic see the *Experts* and the *Statistics* sections in **Sources**, and the earlier chapter on *Propaganda*.

IMPOSED, PERSISTENT AND INGRAINED

Imposed

Imposed authority is the rule of emperors, kings, tsars, khans, shahs and their modern equivalents—those whose word becomes law and whose power is backed by force. These rulers don't govern by consent but by threat, dressing their violence in ceremony and tradition, disguised as the rule of law.

In modern democracies, *imposed authority* is often experienced only in limited forms, so many people have no sense of the relentless oppression that weighs on those under authoritarian rule. In such systems, the *rulers* are the final authority. *You obey*, regardless of how much your decisions, life, possessions and work are taken away from you—or you are beaten, or imprisoned, or killed. Resistance is met with punishment, for both you and your family, as a warning to others. Remember the crucifixions on the roads leading up to Roman-held cities, or the 6000 slaves in Greece. You submit or suffer.

Under imposed regimes, bullies rule absolutely, parasites drain freely, and slaves pay the price with their labor and lives. It's a bitter truth of history—and still reality in much of the world. We must work to undo it.

Persistent

When you experience or witness modern authoritarian regimes—through invasion or government overthrow—you hope the ugliness and oppression will be temporary. That somehow it will be undone. That a better day will dawn. The hope continues, even if small.

But when regimes persist for generations, the original cruelty and murder that built them fades into the past. The victims are forgotten. The conquerors' descendants are crowned kings and queens; the descendants of the conquered serve them. For those in power, the titles vary, but the foundation remains: wealth and power built on theft and conquest.

Many rulers claim the "divine right of kings," imagining themselves accountable only to God. This isn't a metaphor—it's the literal language used to describe such dynasties, rooted in the ancient notion that powerful rulers *were* gods. It is not only a pompous self-delusion, but it works: It keeps the "common people" in place.

Let's tell the truth plainly: Today's nobles inherited wealth built on violence, murder and theft. They have vast fortunes *stolen from the ancestors of their present-day workers*. If you live today under a monarchy anywhere in the world, that means you.

The irony in all this? We're still fascinated by, and respect, those who now hold those stolen fortunes. Consider England, Spain, Sweden, Japan, Jordan, Saudi Arabia, Thailand or a dozen other modern-day kingdoms. (And yes, they may be offended when they read this.)

Magazines and societies are dedicated to their genealogy. Parades celebrate them. Their marriages dominate headlines—especially when a "royal" marries a "commoner." We're entranced by the pageantry, the titles, the fancy clothes, the spectacle. But it's camouflage. Their privilege was stolen from our ancestors—and *persists* at our expense.

Ingrained

My brother-in-law once worked in the mansion of a famous, wealthy actress. "The help" had strict orders to turn their heads and avoid eye contact whenever she was present. And no speaking unless spoken to.

Fame does have its costs. Celebrities are often mobbed, their privacy under constant siege. So boundaries are put in place to manage the chaos.

The symptom with "the help," however, displays something more troubling: an assumed superiority of one class, or caste, above another, and the need for the lower beings to know their place and "show respect."

Mutual respect builds relationships. It's the foundation of reconciliation, friendship, cooperation—even peace between nations. It's essential to *mutual care*.

When one group is required to show deference to its "superiors," it's a hallmark of bullying. It signals a deeper sickness: a culture where inequality is normalized and obedience is expected. Over time, this bullying dynamic gets woven into the social fabric. The "lessers" are trained to serve and submit—often believing it's their rightful place, as if ordained by God or nature. The "betters" expect that submission as natural. It begins to feel inevitable.

Overthrown and Replaced (By Revolution or Rejection)

The rejection of bullies and their imposed authority is hardly new. Some, like Spartacus, failed, and many died in the effort. Other rebellions against imposed authority, though halting, messy and violent, have ultimately resulted in cultures that are profoundly more equitable than the ones overturned—the American and French revolutions are recent examples, as well as many now-independent states in Eastern Europe, Africa and Asia.

But in many cases, revolution just replaced one bully with another—followed by retribution against anyone linked to the prior regime.

Still others, starting with high hopes and promises of justice, grew addicted to power and became bullies and parasites themselves, launching purges and revenge against enemies, whether real, imagined, invented or convenient. Rather than implement an era of fairness to all, they instead simply replaced the previous tyranny with their own.

Every new regime comes dressed in new language and promises of fairness and "a new day ahead"—but it's often the same old structure with new bullies at the top.

Those who promise to be ruthless *for* you will be ruthless *to* you once they gain power. The real failure of socialism, communism and capitalism isn't the system—it's letting wolves replace wolves. Predators always serve themselves. From the schoolyard to the palace, we treat bullies like gods—and they agree.

Closer to Home

Such failures aren't limited to bloody revolutions or national power struggles. The same vices and seductions are rife in society, in families, local politics, homeowners associations, gardening clubs, school boards and religious denominations.

A wronged individual or group protests, organizes and eventually overcomes the bullies—real or perceived—who held power. They'll then wield whatever levers of power are available to punish former opponents—or even bystanders. Public shunning, shaming, fines, permit denials, access blocking, firing, even arrests—whatever tools are at hand.

Should bullies be resisted and restrained? Of course. But when those who win against them simply become the new bullies, everyone loses.

Imposed, persistent and ingrained authority is not solved by swapping out the bully. Never trust a wolf who claims he's there to protect the sheep. In both large and local conflicts, we must see the character and methods of the predators—bully or parasite—and replace them with leaders deeply committed to *action* toward *mutual* care.

GRANTED (CONSENTED TO OR ACCEPTED)

The most valuable—and least understood—form of authority is *granted*: power given by consent. Here, authority is not imposed but accepted by those being led—the "consent of the governed." This idea is equally revolutionary and *essential* to that of the "unalienable rights" of the individual. *Consent* of the governed means an utter rejection of authority *imposed* by a bully, or by any "divine right" to direct the lives of others.

It's also the cornerstone of mutual care. Slaves are forced to work, but they do so unwillingly and under threat. In mutual care, where we agree to work together for each other's benefit, we work harder and more creatively, and we *prosper together* from that effort. When we grant authority for our shared good, the work—and the relationships—are different. That kind of authority is supervisory, not imposed, and benefits all—not just the ones in charge.

THE MODEL OF MUTUAL CARE

The good life is one inspired by love and guided by knowledge.
– Bertrand Russell, "What I Believe" (1925)

Here's the basic pattern of authority in a society created for mutual care: We consent to the *expert* authority who chooses the seeds and directs the timing of planting and harvesting, and we consent to the *supervisor* who *assigns* and *oversees* the various complex and extensive duties needed to plant, tend and harvest. The supervisory authority is genuine and directive, but it is granted by us, consented to, and we all benefit from it.

Clearly there are ways that granted authority can fail or be abused. But mutual care relies on expertise and supervision—experience and social wisdom—to coordinate *shared efforts* for the best outcome.

The authority is *granted* by us, not *imposed* on us. We elect leaders with knowledge and skill, not bullies who impose their will. This is the basic model and genius of *representative democracy*. We *elect* local and national supervisors to coordinate our common life and work. We give them power to govern—and we expect them to use it for everyone's benefit. If they fail, prove corrupt or inept, we vote them out.

It's messy, because bullies and parasites will attempt to manipulate any system to serve themselves. Their goal is *always* to benefit themselves at others' expense. Bullies, Parasites and Slaves—the BPS model—always repeats: take, exploit, hoard.

Any effort by humans to do something together will be complex, because *we* are complex. But avoiding becoming slaves once again means always resisting and restraining bullies and parasites, most especially those that pretend to be our friends, allies and advocates. Which means *seeing* them where they are and *knowing* how they work. And then *refusing* to concede an inch to them.

Our standard for our leaders—those we *entrust* with authority—must always be *mutual care*. If they work well for the good of all, we celebrate their leadership. If they fail, we replace them with *only* those who will champion and enable mutual care—*our rights and needs*, fulfilled by *our obligations and abilities*. This is the wisdom of loving. This must always be our model.

We must ask of every law and initiative: *Does it foster mutual care?* Does it fulfill our shared *needs*—for food, clothing, housing, health, education, safety? Does it affirm our *obligations* to each other? Fulfilling both, needs and obligations, creates the greatest prosperity for all.

That's the test.

It follows that there will be laws and leaders from whom we must withhold consent, and initiate protest, civil disobedience, refusing to obey unjust laws or participate in corrupt systems. This is a legitimate exercise of the rights of the governed, when those rights are threatened or denied. We use them to challenge and remove what threatens our mutual care.

And finally, use this as a lens at the ballot box, to judge the proposals and individuals that seek your consent. *Withhold it* if they don't measure up. *Grant it* only if they do.

UPHOLDING DEMOCRACY

The revolutionary idea of *democracy* was that people got a vote in who led them and what standards they would agree to. Consent of the governed.

There have always been smaller and limited versions of this in history, but applying it to large populations over wide territories was—and remains—revolutionary. That's democracy: *government* by the *consent* of the *governed*. It has its flaws and failures to be sure, but at its core is the moral imperative that people should have a say in how they live—rather than being ruled by bullies, no matter how grand their titles.

For democracy to work, those that participate in it must know and uphold the fundamental values of its government: not just the right to vote, to consent to leaders and laws, but also the foundations on which those stand. That is, we must clearly define those rights and obligations which *constitute* our country's norms, and to which all leaders and laws must conform. That's called a *constitution*. It upholds the rights and obligations of our democracy.

When we raise children, or in small groups, we can share and reinforce our values orally, even generation to generation, "this is who we are and what we believe." But much more is needed for a widely dispersed and diverse nation—or world—if our core values are to be understood and transmitted clearly and consistently. A constitution does this. Of course we need to be wise about what it says, and how it can be interpreted and evolve, but it gives substance to our values and hopes.

Economic Systems

Separate from *governmental* systems (democracies, monarchies, tribes, religions…) there are *economic* systems—and theories about them and how they *should* operate. These are models for organizing how people live and work, often to serve a ruling class, a favored group, or ideally, the common good.

I'll mention five major economic systems here—not to describe them fully, but merely to give a quick picture of what each purports to be, so we can then look at them in relation to the *common* good, and especially to *mutual care*. Without understanding these distinctions, we can be too easily fooled by wild claims, misdirection and propaganda about any of them.

A *really* important distinction: Democracy is not an *economic* system. It's a method of determining leadership and supervision, *governance*, and it can and does coexist with various economic systems in diverse countries around the world.

We can usefully debate which economic systems are most effective, productive or equitable, but we shouldn't confuse them with how leadership is put in place or governs. Both are important, and correlated, but they are different categories of organization, different dimensions of our common life. (More detail on government and economic structures at *Organizing Ourselves* in **Sources**.)

Two Ancient Economic Systems

- ### Hunter-Gatherer / Farming

The oldest economic system is the Hunter-Gatherer model—typically based in families or tribes—and its evolution into Farming, where families plant, harvest, and raise animals for themselves or in cooperation with others. These systems still exist in isolated parts of the world, where contact with larger societies is limited or avoided. Leadership varies: sometimes hereditary, sometimes chosen, sometimes imposed. And yes, bullies, parasites and slaves appear here too. The romanticized "noble savage" is a largely Western fiction.

- ### Feudalism

Feudalism, the most widespread large-scale economic system in history, centers on landowners and serfs. The serfs live and labor on the land but own little or nothing. This is a common model worldwide and throughout history, and the bullies, parasites and slaves are readily visible in its structure. This pattern—of domination and dependency—has repeated in plantations, indentured servitude, sharecropping, trafficking, and monarchies everywhere.

Three New Economic Systems

In contrast to these ancient models, three relatively modern systems—Socialism, Communism and Capitalism—have been defined and attempted. These terms are now so overused and misapplied that they've lost clarity in public discourse. So let's quickly define their core ideas before we examine them more closely.

- ### Socialism

Socialism is *defined* as an economic system where the major and vital industries are owned collectively, that is, by the government (i.e. "by the people"), and decisions are made by elected or appointed officials without personal reward to the officials. In other words, personal profit doesn't drive or influence the decisions—just an objective evaluation of needs and resources. Ownership of smaller or non-critical businesses is permitted and even fostered, but subject to regulations that help ensure fairness and the common good.

- o **COMMUNISM**

Communism is *defined* as an economic system where all the means of production, even of non-major and non-vital industries, are owned collectively, by the government (or "The State"), and all decisions are made by elected or appointed officials without personal reward based on their outcomes. Local officials may oversee businesses and make decisions, but they do not own or profit from them personally.

- o **CAPITALISM**

Capitalism is *defined* as an economic system where owners and investors control production, and profit is the primary motive. Decisions are made not by public officials, but by those with "capital"—*money* and the power that comes with it. Hence the name.

Those are the three dominant modern theories of economic systems. We can argue about the successes and failures of each—and we should—but those are the plain definitions and basic theories of each. In reality, no country fully conforms to any of these three economic systems. Each incorporates elements of the others.

Even during the most draconian phases of communism under Stalin and Mao, "The State" never fully achieved total control. It and its leaders simply could not and did not control everyone everywhere—though they tried! Entrepreneurs eventually emerged and launched their own businesses. Today, both Russia and China are home to billionaire capitalists who influence, and sometimes direct, government decisions. They may fight at times, but make no mistake: *Capitalism is very much alive* in so-called communist countries.

A number of other countries declare themselves to be socialist, and implement this to a greater or lesser degree, but in these as well, small and large entrepreneurs own and run businesses, and billionaires are present and highly influential. *Capitalism also lives* in socialist countries.

Even in capitalist nations, governments typically own or regulate major sectors—armed forces, transportation, healthcare, food safety and more. These regulations aim to ensure justice and public safety. In that sense, elements of socialism and communism are embedded in capitalist systems.

In practice, every system is messier than its definition. All three economic models allow for ambition and entrepreneurship—especially when it serves those in power. *Every* country blends aspects of socialism, communism, and capitalism, though usually one is dominant.

It's a lot to take in, but it helps us think more clearly about what's broken in our own *capitalist* system. Capitalism nurtures creativity and entrepreneurship—but we must also face its failures honestly. One of the greatest is its frequent neglect of mutual care. Let's look at that now.

ECONOMIC SYSTEMS, DEMOCRACY AND MUTUAL CARE

First, let's observe that any economic system can be chosen and function by the democratic election of government leaders. And any economic system can be imposed by bullies, drained by parasites, and then exploit slaves to do all the actual work.

As much as we might rail against the evils of communism, socialism or capitalism, our complaints usually come down to this: how they are *exploited* by people willing to advance their own interests through force and deception. It's always about the bullies and parasites—who steal, twist and manipulate *any* economic system to suit themselves.

One of the go-to accusations by bullies and parasites who are thriving within a capitalist economic system is that any movement toward *mutual care* and the *common* good arises from socialists or communists and therefore must be rejected outright. They claim:

- Wage inequity may hurt those at the bottom—who can't afford housing, food, healthcare, or education—but that's *how* capitalism *works*. Everyone has a *chance* to rise, but you're on your own.
- If some are denied equal healthcare, or suffer because the insurance company refused a medicine or procedure, we're told it's the unavoidable means to profits, and limits dependency and abuse. *Profits*, they claim, are the only way we can attract good leaders and investors. They *incentivize* the market. They make it *work*.

I know these claims sound outrageous when stated so plainly. But even dressed in polished language or academic theory, they're exactly what we're *told to believe*—and why we're taught to *fear* any effort toward mutual care. The basic lie is this: "To keep capitalism strong, some must naturally suffer poverty wages and ill health, but they have the *opportunity* to lift themselves up and out."

I once bought that idea as good economic theory—unfortunate realities necessary for capitalism's success.

I'm an avowed capitalist. Read my résumé. I've been starting and running businesses since I was twelve. But I do not believe in that flawed version of capitalism anymore. It's the same twisted, evil logic as sacrificing children to get a good harvest: Some must *suffer* so others can *prosper*. It's not just wrong—it's *monstrous*. The moment we see it clearly, we're accountable. **It must be stopped.**

So what can we do about it? Here's how we fix it…

Within a capitalist economy, we can carve out areas that are *intentionally* profit-free—especially where profit motives would deprive people of what they *need*.

It is unwise to tempt *any* decision-makers to choose between increasing their own incomes and ensuring the care of others.

Dismissing mutual care with scare words isn't an argument—it's either ignorance or manipulation.

Yes, socialism and communism claim, and perhaps attempt, to provide mutual care.

Does that make mutual care bad or wrong? No.

Mutual care is wise—and we have the means, knowledge, and logistics to make it work. Ensuring food, housing, health, education, and safety for *everyone* helps us be our best, *most productive* selves. And that brings abundance and thriving.

Logically then, if profit motives ever conflict with meeting our common needs, the needs must win. That's just common sense. It's capitalism with a moral backbone and a wise heart, building a better, beautiful future. That's why mutual care is imperative.

When it comes to non-essentials—fancy clothes, gadgets, even spaceships—make all the profit you want! Let capitalism reign and income rain! The next billionaire could be you or me—as long as we don't steal from others, bully the weak, or make anyone a slave.

It is perfectly moral and acceptable for some to strive and become wealthy.

Just don't do it by diverting funds needed for mutual care into anyone's pocket.

We can't allow that anymore.

How to Train Up True Leaders

Bully leaders sacrifice others to benefit themselves—through ambition, theft, self-flattery, conquest, revenge and cruelty.

True leaders sacrifice of themselves to benefit others—giving their talents, resources—sometimes even their lives. They model what it is to care for others. The cooperative action they inspire yields far more than the forced labor of those who are exploited and under the lash.

But true leaders are trained up, not just born that way. From a very early age, they're taught *empathy*—how to *see the needs* of others as *real* and *vital*, and to act accordingly. Meeting those needs fully is key to having our own needs fully met. Only with this kind of wisdom and compassion can leaders be equipped to coordinate our common work.

Bullying often masquerades as "being in charge," even from childhood—so early training and modeling really matters.

Some may be born with leadership capacity, but without the intentional teaching of empathy, it will be crippled and misused. Anything less leads us back to bullying.

I began this book with the statement, **"We need a hard reset on who we are, and who we allow to lead us."**

"Who we are" is about moral and rational decision-making, and the evolutionary imperative to fulfill common rights and needs through common obligations and abilities. Simply put, we must **replace exploitation with mutual care** as the highest value and necessity for our common life. Let that be who we are.

"Who we allow to lead us" is about coordinated action. Once we commit to mutual care, we must *organize* to live it. That requires leadership.

At every level—from cleaning up a park to freeing refugees or governing a nation—leadership means skilled supervision: wisely organizing and managing others to get something done. We need to recognize and acknowledge our *widespread, systemic failure* across leadership of government, business, healthcare, retail, even our families: We lack *good* supervision.

We *have* supervision nearly everywhere. Supervision is the singular ability required of any leader in any position at any level. But it is often dreadful, from bad motives, skills or training.

We know good supervision when we experience it, but even leadership courses often miss key essentials and elevate or excuse bullying.

Let's reflect together. Take this opportunity to recall your own experiences supervising or being supervised. That wisdom can benefit all of us going forward, in our mutual care for one another. The two online sites, **BPS.online** and **MutualCare.online**, provide a means for *you* to share for our common benefit.

I've worked at almost every level of supervision in my life: from being at the bottom and being bossed around by irritable managers in construction and retail, to middle management with supervisors above me and employees below me, to CEO of a national company, senior vice-president of an international company, and also as the pastor of a small, multi-ethnic congregation. I started businesses as small as cutting lawns in my neighborhood. I delivered newspapers. I cleaned offices after hours. I did spot-welding in a factory. I worked a hospital's graveyard shift. I worked in recording studios and led a band. I edited magazines…

It's a bunch, I know. We all wish that boy could just focus for a while.

What I learned through it all was the nature of good leadership. I saw supervision at every level—some excellent, much of it poor. As I advanced, I tried to avoid the bad, model the good, and teach what worked. It was always a challenge.

Whether you're a team leader of a small cleaning crew or the president of a country, one of the constant realities of being a supervisor is that when you supervise others, no matter how pure your motives or reasonable your decisions, someone will malign either or both.

People who weren't present at meetings or events may presume or pretend they know what was said or done—and present those assumptions as fact. Some will hold onto resentment and spread accusations you can't easily disprove. Simply denying them just fuels suspicion. Instead, clarify what you can, keep records, invite transparency, and let consistent integrity be your strongest defense.

To be clear, that's not me grumbling as some sort of victim. I'm describing a standard reality of leadership, and if you aspire to lead, know this: You will be attacked—to your face or behind your back. Some of it will be for actual errors—we all make them—and some will be simply made up to hurt you. Out of competition, jealousy or… "who knows what evil lurks in the hearts of men?"

This opposition will rise and fall, but it will never vanish. If you're considering leadership, know this: *Opposition comes with the job.*

When I retired from my last position, I remember saying, "I want to keep being useful. I'll write, speak out, maybe teach. I just don't want to be in charge of anything anymore." That sentiment came from experience. Being in charge is hard work, and the more people and responsibility you have, the harder it gets. The biggest challenge isn't public speaking, vision, strategy, finance or organizational charts. The real challenge is *the people* you oversee. Day in and day out, it's people.

It's called *super-vision* for a reason—to *see over*. Whether managing a mission to Mars or a stock room, the role is to *see* what's needed and coordinate *the people you lead* to get it done. That's why someone is placed in charge—to see the need and guide us toward it—together.

Bully leaders—from retail supervisors to CEOs, presidents and monarchs—rely on command alone, indifferent to how their orders affect real people. To them, workers are chess pieces. They're not led to achieve goals—they're *pushed around*—and sacrificed if needed.

This is the bully model. It is the opposite of mutual care. It fails because it exploits and enslaves. The labels change, but the model does not.

People "bossed" this way—under the lash—don't thrive. They *survive* just enough to get through the day and maybe pay the bills, if even that. They're often treated with suspicion and contempt: "They'll get away with anything they can." And they end up fulfilling this low expectation, because *mistreatment creates mistrust.*

By contrast, gifted supervisors ask themselves, and their employees, "What can I do to make you successful in your job, and to make us successful together?" They don't revel in pride of position or refuse to seek counsel from those they lead. They *lead* to achieve goals.

In fact, good supervisors listen—especially to the people doing the work. If there's a real problem or better solution, they want to know! And "whistleblowers" are rewarded, not punished. Hiding problems is what bullies and parasites do, not good supervisors.

Good supervisors, true leaders, also strive to provide opportunity to all those they lead: for advancement, education, recognition. Better skills, greater satisfaction—better results. All of these contribute to our shared prosperity. The more we all grow, the more we all gain.

Not Everyone Is a Supervisor...

And note this important reality check: not everyone is blessed with the skill of *supervision*. Those who are *help us work together* toward a common goal. But countless *other talents* are just as vital—and deserve *equal recognition and reward*. Supervision must not be the only test for, or path toward, advancement.

A German cartoonist, Hans Traxler, well-illustrated the error of judging all abilities by a single standard back in 1983. It was redrawn and put into English by the New Zealand cartoonist Barry Linton in 2000 and has been widely circulated online because of its scathing insight.

In it, a crow, a monkey, a penguin, an elephant, a goldfish, a seal and a dog, all stand with a tree behind them. An examiner at a desk in front of them says, "For a fair selection everybody has to take the same exam: Please climb that tree." (The cartoon is linked in ***Sources***.)

This cartoon reminds us: Every gift, ability and skill needs its own opportunities. Skills should be rewarded as they become increasingly valuable to our common good. This is both moral and wise.

When only *supervision* is well-rewarded, it attracts even those not gifted, who often imitate the *worst* examples of supervision they've seen or experienced. When *all abilities* are rewarded, people naturally are drawn to and advance in the areas where they best produce good results.

Too often, organizations reward people primarily based on how many subordinates they have—especially close to the top, where pay becomes wildly disproportionate and morally compromised—as we saw with the examples of retail and healthcare executives and their compensations.

As an executive, you may direct and lead many people below you, but your daily job is typically supervising a small number of *direct* reports—who supervise others in turn, and so on down the chart. You may get to a "higher level" in the hierarchy, but your supervisory duties remain about the same regardless of level—you personally directly lead a handful of people. This simple truth should help us gauge compensation more wisely, instead of letting senior leaders overpay themselves and underpay those at the bottom.

This brings us to the deeper question of what leadership really reveals—not just in systems, but in people themselves. Consider this exchange between Marilyn Vos Savant, a renowned thinker and writer, and a reader, who sent this question to her weekly column...

Dear Marilyn: How do you tell the difference between good and evil?
Dear Reader: You give it power.

This cuts to the core of leadership. Power is a test. Give someone authority, and watch what they do with it. Do they abuse it, or use it to lift others up? Do their instincts tilt toward self-gain or shared well-being—toward exploitation or care?

This is the crucible of leadership—power doesn't create character; it reveals it. And when we choose our leaders, this must be our standard. This is the core of mutual care in leadership. Not what someone *promises* when still powerless, but what they *do* once power is in their hands.

SUPERVISION AND MUTUAL CARE

The best supervisors actually care about those they lead, and they show it, both by *actions* and *attitude*—and these *inspire* those they supervise *to rise to the challenges*, and even to ask, "What else can I do?" They also ensure that *all* those they lead are *well* and *fairly* compensated. It is the reason why productivity and job satisfaction are typically higher in employee-owned businesses. When everyone has a mutual stake, and all are treated well, everyone thrives. **This** kind of supervision is essential to mutual care. It creates more abundance than the bully model, where the exploited give the bare minimum just to survive.

> **An imbalance between rich and poor is the oldest and most fatal ailment of all republics. – Plutarch**

Look with suspicion on models of leadership that look to bullies of the past or present for their methods. Throw those methods away. They are poison to our common life and threaten our future together. It's time we judge leadership not by domination, but by care.

All true leadership, at any scale, is rooted in mutual care.

(A wealth of literature on this is under *Servant Leadership* in **Sources**.)

COORDINATED ACTION

Throughout history, there have always been bullies—those who stole and hoarded the abundance of others for their own gain. But for all their self-glory, every one of them and their kingdoms fell and were replaced. Predators get consumed by other predators. They are not fit to lead, rule or survive. They are an evolutionary dead-end.

Parasites have long praised these bullies, fed off them and their victims and passed down ruthless methods for retaining power and expanding kingdoms—methods that kill or crush anyone seen as a burden or threat.

They glorified death and cruelty and called it honor and power. But their words and deeds reveal who they truly are. They need not be named again, nor regarded for their infamy, except as object lessons of failure. Let their excesses expose their theft, for what they built was not *earned* but *stolen*.

Against such villainy stands a simple evolutionary imperative: *mutual care*. Your well-being is best protected when everyone's well-being is.

This insight has been voiced in many forms over millennia by the greatest philosophers and religious leaders. It is the core principle of true civilization. The evidence is all around us: Some organisms are better equipped to survive environmental challenges than others. It is witnessed throughout all orders of life on earth—from bacteria to fish, birds, animals and people. That's *an* insight of "evolution," and it's not wrong.

The error arises when this insight is misapplied to human leadership—especially the false idea that "apex predators" are the fittest to rule. This view fails on several counts. It imagines that predation—even against one's own species—is the highest form of survival. That victims are nature's design. That we can do nothing about it. None of this is true.

There is another factor that changes outcome: *coordinated action*. Evolution is *not* fate or predestination. We're not mindless products of a capricious environment, nor helpless against predators or storms.

Many organisms use coordinated action to adapt to or protect themselves from their environment, or to defend against predators. Ants build colonies. Birds migrate in formation. Wolves hunt in packs. These shared efforts improve their survival. Coordinated action makes them more fit to thrive. They don't dominate alone—they thrive together.

We humans do this constantly. It's why we wear clothing, build homes, establish farms and hospitals, and construct vast transportation networks. It's why we've done so well against natural dangers and predators. It's why we worry about global warming, arrest conmen, and have a standing army for defense against would-be conquerors.

Our *coordinated action* brought us to the level of technology and civilization we now enjoy. Despite our conflicts and flaws, it is this collaboration—not solitary strength—that has created our abundance.

And yet, in the midst of this, robbers and conmen still take more than they deserve—and claim credit for what we built together. The slaves do the work, and the bullies take the praise. The parasites steal from the shadows.

Our coordinated action did not succeed because a bully forced us to work. It succeeded because we worked.

The foundational truth of coordinated action is that it *is* mutual care. By working with each other and for our common good, we all thrive.

But let's be practical: Coordinated action depends on both *expertise* and *supervision*. It does not require "leadership" from those who seize power through violence or intimidation. Nor from those who quietly siphon off others' work and call it their own. Those who steal and hoard are unfit to lead. They must be resisted and restrained.

Only those who act and lead in service of mutual care are qualified. Mutual care is the coordinated action that enables us to survive and prosper. It is our *evolutionary imperative*.

This simple wisdom—treating others the way we want to be treated—is not just a moral good. It is a practical key to our future. And the Golden Rule isn't a naïve sentiment. It is the foundation of prosperity, of a wonderful future for us, our children, and our children's children, in which no one is exploited, excluded or left behind.

When food, clothing, shelter, healthcare, education and safety are provided to all without exception—by our *mutual care* for each other—we all rise together. That is why we *need* it.

Replacing *exploitation* with *mutual care*. That is our call, our duty, and our only real hope for the future.

Let's make it so.

WHAT YOU CAN DO NOW

- **BULLIES AND PARASITES**
- Recognize that some take and hoard by force and deception.
- Call them what they are: bullies and parasites.
- Stop honoring or celebrating them—in history or today.
- If you are one, stop.
- If you see one, expose it.
- Refuse to go along. Resist and restrain them.
- Use every nonviolent means—legislation, protest, persuasion, teaching—to expose and stop them.
- Change the laws, leaders and systems that hold others down.

- **SLAVES**
- Recognize that some lives have been exploited to subsidize bullies and parasites. Call them what they have been forced to be: slaves.
- Stop the exploitation. Free those who are bound.
- Ensure justice for those who have been taken from.
- Reward honest work with honest pay, and increased effort and skill with increased reward.
- If you've been exploited, speak up. Your story matters. Share your truth to help break the cycle of exploitation.

- **MUTUAL CARE**
- Recognize the Golden Rule: Common needs require common obligations. For each, from each.
- Enact laws that meet common needs by common obligation.
- Repeal laws that benefit some by the suffering of others.
- Ensure no one gains by denying others what they need.
- Reject dismissive labels. Affirm the one we truly need: *mutual care*.
- Foster all abilities and skills—create a better world together.
- Ensure food, shelter, healthcare, education and safety for everyone.
- Help others thrive by ensuring thriving for all.
- Guarantee equal justice. If one is at risk, all are.
- Reward extraordinary achievement for those who create—but never at the cost of basic human needs.
- Care for others. Teach others to care.
- Use your talents, time, fortune and creativity to lift others.
- Honor and celebrate those who embody the Golden Rule.

- ○ **OUR EVOLUTIONARY IMPERATIVE**
  - Mutual care—not exploitation—is what ensures our survival and prosperity. We *can* replace human exploitation with mutual care. It is our evolutionary imperative. ***We can do it. We must.***
  - Mutual care brings thriving and abundance for all. Its time has come.
  - ***Do it. Persist in it.***

Resources and expanded topics are at **BPS.online**. Our first shared task is to systematically expose how bullies and parasites steal—*who* they are, *how* they operate and *how* we resist them. This QR code will take you there:

The more we are all aware of the devices and disguises of bullies and parasites, and the social, political and economic systems they manipulate, the more we can strive *to free each other* from their exploitation.

We will use this freedom to care for each other instead, to bring thriving and abundance for all of us. Extensive and growing resources for that as well are at **MutualCare.online**. This QR code will take you there:

The two sites are tightly linked, and free. Come aboard, and join your abilities to all of ours, for creating true *mutual care*. We must.

ABOUT THE AUTHOR

I hate that I live in a world where I must write this book. I hate that this book needs to be written. I dearly hope that by reading this book, you'll see what to hate—and halt it. And also see what to do, and do it, for each other, for our future together.

I wrote this short poem decades ago. It received diverse circulation, copies and reprints in many publications. I affirm it still, for individuals, and for groups who live in silos, who think alike and isolate themselves from others.

Who Think Alone Grow Peculiar

Who think alone grow peculiar,
their minds unchastened
by friend, foe and
the normal humdrum of the outer world.
Ideas sprung half-formed,
standing on ideas sprung
half-formed, the acrobats locked,
veering, threatened by any,
loudly defensive of their monstrosity,
unaware of its error,
repulsed by the world where seen.
Less secure, less complete,
less consistent is the commerce of ideas,
the battle of wits, the slurry of abuse
and success in the world, and more true.
We stand better on the shoulders of others
than on our own.
   – George Byron Koch, 1983

In virtually every area of life, social, political, religious, scientific, moral and cultural, I have held ideas one way, then changed sides—sometimes more than once. I've discovered there aren't just two sides, but many—and entire areas where no one really has any idea.

The message of *Bullies, Parasites and Slaves: Replacing Exploitation With Mutual Care* has to stand or fall on its own. But it's also true that the conclusions reached here flow from decades of observations, decisions, debates, faiths, friendships, skepticism, history, science, people, logic, books, family, travel, and sitting quietly lost in thought. This mix lobbies against easy labels like *conservative*, *liberal*, *moderate*—or any of the thousand other social, political and religious boxes we assign each other as we each try to understand and organize our human experiences in this universe.

It's complicated, right?

My alliances and choices over the years have puzzled many partisans of one camp or another: I've sided with the one being treated inequitably—even when I didn't fully agree with them. But I don't therefore believe in unthinking acceptance of every style and manner of life. Some are unhealthy, some evil-hearted, some meaningless, some neutral, and some loving, caring, fun-filled, joyful and vital. Most are several of those all at once. I might even disagree with choices of lifestyle, faith or culture, while affirming the right to live it—unless it harms or exploits others. Then I will resist and restrain it.

Some may find pleasure in insulting or taking advantage of others. I believe both are damaging to our common future. Hence this book.

You can chase down a fuller biography and access to my other books, talks, music, and artwork at **BPS.online**, under *Author*. In the end, all of it—thought, art, struggle, speech and writing—is for one reason: to help us to care for each other.

You've heard my story and my insights, seen my puzzle pieces of reality assembled before your eyes, and now the picture should be clear: Mutual care is the one solution open to us.

Now it's your turn to make it real.

GLOSSARY OF TERMS

This Glossary includes terms used throughout the book. It goes beyond basic definitions to explain some of the book's foundational ideas. Entries are organized alphabetically by word or phrase, not by chapter. **Bolded** terms within definitions indicate cross-references to other entries.

Advocacy. Working in support of a particular cause or policy.
Agnostic. Someone who doubts the existence of God or the supernatural, but does not deny the possibility.
Allegations. A claim that someone has done something wrong.
Alleged. A claim about someone or something, that may or may not be proven.
Amulet. A small item or piece of jewelry believed to protect against danger or disease.
Anarchist. A person who advocates or promotes anarchy, or the overthrow of existing government or social order.
Anarchy. A state of chaos or disorder in the social order or government.
Ankh. An object used in ancient Egypt as a symbol of life, similar to a cross but with a loop at the top.
Annul. Cancel or declare invalid an agreement or decision.
Apex Predator. A **predator** at the top of a food chain, usually without natural predators of its own, but subject to conflict with others of its own species.
Apologetics. Arguments or writings in rational justification of a theory or religious doctrine.
Apologist. A person who presents an argument in defense of something.
Apostasy. Technically the renunciation of a religious or political belief, but in common usage an accusation or label for those who don't agree with a particular belief.
Apostolic. Following in a line of succession of those who are in authority of a particular religious system, most commonly Christianity.
Aryan. In Nazi ideology, denoting "white" non-Jewish people, especially of northern European origin, and typically having blond hair and blue eyes, and a supposedly superior "racial" group.
Atheist. Someone who denies the existence of God or the supernatural, typically by acknowledging no evidence to support such beliefs.
Authoritarian. Promoting or enforcing strict obedience to authority, especially that of leaders or the government, and at the cost of personal freedom.
Autocrat/Autocratic. A ruler who has absolute directive power, without accountability to the law or those who are governed.
Aztec. A member of an **indigenous** people's group in Mexico before the Spanish conquest of the 16th century.
B.C.E. An abbreviation for "Before Common Era." Used typically in academic, secular and non-Christian publications to refer to the years before the birth of Jesus Christ. "C.E." refers to the years following.
Banality. So lacking in originality as to be both obvious and boring.

Blacklists. A list of people or things that are regarded by those in power to be unacceptable or untrustworthy, and therefore to be prohibited or avoided.
Blasphemy. Technically the offense of speaking **sacrilegiously** about God or sacred things, but used commonly to disparage a disagreeable opinion.
Bolshevik. Russian for "bigger." A member of the Russian Social Democratic Party, renamed the Communist Party after seizing power in the October Revolution of 1917. Also used as a slander against those in other countries who advocate common care.
Bribery. Persuading another to make a decision or commit an act, typically illegally or dishonestly, by a gift of money or other favors.
Bully. A person who takes advantage of others, typically with threat of harm, law or other means.
Bureaucrat. Someone working in a **bureaucracy**.
Bureaucracy. A system of government in which day-to-day organizational and governance decisions are made by employees and appointees of local, regional or national agencies, rather than directly by elected representatives.
Capitalism. An economic system in which trade and industries are controlled by private owners through the investment of capital (money), typically for profit.
Capricious. Decisions based on mood, emotion or other non-rational means, and often at odds with or uninterested in facts or experience.
Caricature. A drawing, description or imitation of a person, thing or idea, in which certain characteristics are exaggerated or invented, to create humor, slander or disgust.
Cartel. An alliance of manufacturers, suppliers or distributors with the purpose of controlling prices and restricting competition. These range from corporations to governments to gangs.
Catfishing. Creating a fake online identity to con people into believing they are friends, or romantically interested in them, with the goal of theft or control. A form of scam. Catfishers use images of other people, personal info and a fictional persona to fool victims.
Class warfare. An idea propounded by Marx, Engels, Stalin, Castro, Mao and others that society is divided into two classes: the working class (the *proletariat*) and the ruling class (the *bourgeoisie*). It advocated for the working class to seize all property and means of production from the ruling class and own them collectively. This idea failed for several reasons, including the complexity of human relationships (e.g., Che Guevara called workers "cogs in the wheel of the state"), the ability of bullies and parasites to exploit any system—even communism—and the simpler possibility of practicing mutual care within any system, including capitalism.
Cold War. A era of political and economic conflict between the U.S. and the Soviet Union from 1947–1991. The term "cold war" denotes a lack of actual military conflict between the two countries. Instead, it was through political and economic battles, **propaganda,** and proxy wars—such as between North and South Vietnam.
Collateral damage. The euphemistic term for the deaths, injuries, or damages done that were not the intended consequence of an action. Blowing up a building to kill one enemy causes collateral damage: the death of other people, the destruction of the building and all of its residences and businesses, and the lasting effect on all of the families and businesses connected to those that died and were destroyed.

Communism. A social structure in which all property is owned *in common* and each person works and receives according to their abilities and needs. The idea dates back to early civilizations, but since the 18th century has taken many forms—from class warfare (Russia, China, Cuba), to religious communes, to extended family systems. The term itself is now so ill-defined as to be nearly useless (and inflammatory) if not rigorously explained in any debate. **Marxism** is one *variant* commonly invoked to create or explain class warfare but itself does not define communism.
Con. Persuade a person or group to do or believe something, often by deception.
Confidence man (or **con man**). A person who steals from someone by gaining their confidence and persuading them willingly to give up money or property.
Conquistador. A conqueror, especially one of the Spanish or Portuguese conquerors of the Caribbean, Mexico, Central and South America, Oceana, Africa and Asia in the 15th and 16th centuries.
Conspiracy. Secretly planning with other people to do something, usually bad or illegal.
Conspiracy theory. A belief that some secret influential and intentional organization is responsible for political, social, scientific events or phenomena. Examples range from the Illuminati, to Big Pharma, to the Deep State, to the Elders of Zion, to Aliens. Are there groups that seek to secretly influence others for their benefit? Yes. Where conspiracy theories fail is in imagining that many powerful people (or aliens) can keep their activities secret. Conspiracy theories also fail by their effect on their believers, isolating them from other ideas, evidence and debate.
Conversion. The act of fraudulently changing the official ownership of property. Theft.
Corruption. Dishonest or fraudulent conduct by those in positions of power, typically by bribery with money or other favors.
Crucifixion. The act of crucifying. See **Crucify**.
Crucify. Putting someone to a cruel and painful death by nailing or binding them to a cross or pole, typically in public view, as an act of punishment and a warning to others. Widely used by Romans and other empires to ensure submission.
Cult. A group of people having beliefs or practices regarded by others as strange, sinister, or simply at odds with knowledge and evidence.
Decimate. Kill, demolish, or remove a large percentage of a population or property.
Deconstruct. To break down a problem or idea into parts, in order to analyze or understand its meaning.
Defame. Damage the reputation of someone or something by slander or lies.
Defraud. Steal property or money by deception.
Dehumanize. By lies and other deceptions, to make any group of human beings seem less valuable than others, usually as a pretext to harm of theft.
Democratic Socialism. A political and economic philosophy supporting both democratic governance and public or state ownership of key industries considered essential to national welfare—such as healthcare, transportation and utilities.
Depravity. Conscious moral corruption or wickedness.
Despot. A ruler who holds absolute power and exercises it in a cruel or oppressive way.
Dialectic. Discussing or considering more than one opinion, in order to arrive at truth, which is often a synthesis rather than simply the choice of one over the other.

Dictator. A ruler with total power over a country or institution, typically who has obtained or maintained it by force.
Dictatorship. A country or institution ruled by a dictator.
Dynasty. People from the same family, usually over generations, with a prominent role in government, business, politics or society.
Dystopia. A state or society in which there is great suffering or injustice. The opposite of a utopia.
Emancipation Proclamation. A document issued by President Abraham Lincoln on January 1, 1863. It declared that enslaved people in the United States, and importantly in the Confederate states, were free.
Embezzle. Steal or misappropriate funds or other property belonging to the people or organization for which one works.
Enlightenment. A movement beginning in Europe in the 17th century, related to the Scientific Revolution, that focused on applying rational and empirical thought to meet the problems of society. These ideas included separation or church and state, progress, tolerance, constitutional government, individual liberty and the pursuit of freedom, knowledge and happiness. Also called the Age of Reason.
Enslavement. The action of making someone a **slave**, by force, captivity, or social and legal restriction; **subjugation**.
Entitlement. Rights granted by law, given by legal "title," like the title to a car or home. Also refers to the belief that someone is deserving of special privileges or treatment for historical or other causes.
Epidemiologist. A specialist or expert in the branch of medicine that deals with the origin, transmission, and medical control of diseases.
Espouse. To claim or support a cause, belief or way of life.
Eugenics. The study of how to manipulate reproduction within a human population to favor certain heritable characteristics. Popularized as a racially biased theory, it was used by the Nazis to justify exterminating Jews, disabled people and other minorities deemed "undesirable."
Euphemism. A word or expression used in place of one considered too harsh or explicit.
Evolution. In biology, the observation that groups of organisms change over time in response to challenges from the environment, where the fittest in a group are most likely to survive and reproduce. Their survival characteristics are thereby passed down to their descendants and become characteristics of a larger and growing group, while those less fit tend to die off over time.
Exploitation. Taking advantage of someone to benefit unfairly from their work.
Expunge. Remove completely.
Extirpation. Completely cutting out, removing or destroying a species or organism from a specific place. Also refers to the removal of something unwanted or bad.
Extort. Obtain something by threat or force.
False narrative. A belief or story based on incorrect, incomplete, merely traditional, or intentionally fabricated information or history.

Fascism. A form of government typically ruled by one ruler or a small group, under a single party, with extreme nationalism, militarism and national interests above those of the individual.

Feudalism. The dominant social system in medieval Europe—and much of world history—in which the "nobility" held lands by the authority of the monarchy, and serfs lived on their "lord's" land and gave obedience, labor and a share of the produce, in exchange for protection.

Genocide. The intentional widespread or complete destruction of a national, ethnic or religious group.

Gentry. People of good social position. In the United Kingdom (England and beyond) the class of people next below the "nobility" in social position.

Ghetto. A poor urban area occupied primarily by a minority group or groups, confined there by social distinctions, poverty or laws.

Gigolo. A young man paid or financially supported by an older person to be an escort or lover. Also used of a con who takes advantage of an older person by pretending to care for them.

Gladiator. In ancient Rome, a man trained to fight with weapons—sometimes to the death—against other men or animals in an arena, for the crowd's entertainment.

Gold-digger. One who forms a relationship with another person to extract money or favors from them.

Golden Circle. Another name for a **Ponzi Scheme**, in which people are recruited to invest money and then to recruit additional people (usually friends and family) to also invest money, and where a fraction of each new investment is paid to those who recruited them, on up the line to the founders. The fraud is that no new money is created, and the process fails mathematically because it runs out of new investors, while those at the very top get rich.

Gussy up. Informal vernacular that means to dress up or decorate something, for a special occasion, or to hide a flaw or fraud.

Hellenize. Relating to Greek history, language, and culture imposed on vast territories, starting from the conquests and reign of Alexander the Great.

Heresy. Belief or opinion contrary to orthodox or commonly held religious (or other) doctrine. From a root meaning simply "to follow a different way."

Heretic. A person believing in or practicing **heresy**.

Hidalgo. Spanish for a gentleman or member of the "nobility."

Human trafficking. The act of transporting or coercing people in order to benefit from their work, in the form of forced labor or sexual exploitation.

Humanism. A worldview giving prime importance to human beings, rather than divine or supernatural matters. Humanists stress the value and potential goodness of human beings, emphasize common needs, and seek only rational (not religious) ways of solving human problems. See **Atheist** and **Agnostic**.

Hyperbole. Exaggerated statements or claims.

Icon. A person or thing regarded as a symbol of an idea or notable person and worthy of veneration or attention.

Imprescriptible rights. Rights that cannot be taken away, lost, or revoked by any person, authority or law. They are permanent, intrinsic, and cannot be forfeited, even if unused for a long time.
Inalienable. Unable to be taken away from, or given away.
Incumbent. An official, party or regime currently holding office.
Indelible. Memories, actions and colors that are impossible to erase, remove or change.
Indentured servitude. A labor contract where a person works for a set period of time, usually to pay off a debt or earn freedom. The contract itself is called an indenture.
Indigenous. Originating or historically present in a particular place; native.
Insidious. Gradual, subtle harm.
Intrinsic. Naturally present; essential.
Inveigh. Speak or write about something with deep hostility.
Jargon. Words or expressions used by a particular profession or group—with special meaning—and are therefore difficult for others to understand.
Kickback. A payment made to a person in power, usually secretly and illegally, for facilitating a transaction, an approval, a license or an appointment to a job.
Lackey. Acting obediently and subserviently for someone in power.
Land baron. A person who owns large amounts of land.
Larceny. Theft of personal property. Stealing.
Largesse. Money or gifts given generously to others.
Liturgy. A framework of actions, words, and music used in church worship or other formal meetings.
Lobbyist. A person who works to attempt to influence legislators and legislation.
Logistics. The detailed coordination of operations, over time, involving many people, facilities and supplies. The entire process of moving raw goods through transportation, manufacturing and delivery of a finished product is all logistics: the logic of coordination.
Long con. A complex, planned, and extended scam that involves tricking people to steal money or take advantage of them.
Lynching. Killing someone, especially by hanging, for an alleged offense with or without a legal trial.
Machiavellian. Cunning, scheming and unscrupulous, especially in politics. The term comes from advice given in the book *The Prince* by 16th-century Italian diplomat and political theorist Niccolò Machiavelli.
Malign. Speak in a malevolently critical manner of someone's character or intentions.
Mark. A targeted victim of theft, either by a con or robbery.
Mayan. The people primarily of the Yucatan, Belize and Guatemala, who had a culture (circa 300 to 900 C.E.) known for its outstanding architecture, pottery and astronomy. Also a family of languages spoken in Central America and Mexico.
Mickey (slipping a). "Spiking" drinks with drugs to induce sleep or weakness. Also called a "roofie."
Militia. Originally, a military force raised from the civilian population to supplement a regular army in an emergency. More recently, an independent military force that engages in actions outside of the structures of a nation's own government and military.

Miscegenation. A racial theory that sexual relationships or reproduction between people of different ethnic groups is immoral and produces inferior offspring. See also **Eugenics**.

Misdirection. Drawing someone's attention to the wrong place or in the wrong direction to hide an act or object.

Multi-Level Marketing (MLM). A sales organization where participants are compensated not just by the sales they make but especially by the number of new salespeople they recruit. Each new salesperson must purchase some of the product as "inventory" and are charged for that purchase. The person who recruited them thereby gets a sales commission on those products, and every person "above" them on the "down line," who recruited them to sell, also gets a percentage of the sale. Though the company's marketing materials make it appear to a legitimate business with products—makeup, storage containers, vitamins—in fact those products often end up in the closets and garages of the salespeople, who can't find buyers, in part because they are trying to recruit new salespeople rather than sell actual products to customers. Shares many characteristics with a **Ponzi scheme**. The founders make a lot of money, and people on the down line end up paying more than they earn.

NAACP. Abbreviation for National Association for the Advancement of Colored People. A civil-rights organization that works to ensure the rights of African-Americans and other minorities in the United States.

Napalm. A highly flammable, sticky jelly used in incendiary bombs and flamethrowers.

Neuron. A type of cell that receives and sends messages within the brain and to and from the body.

New World. A term used by Europeans to describe the Americas after Christopher Columbus' discovery. It was new to them but held indigenous civilizations of great age, which were then enslaved by conquests primarily from Spain and Portugal—also why Spanish and Portuguese are the primary languages South of the United States.

Noble savage. A member of "primitive" humankind when free from the corrupting influence of civilization, as idealized in romantic and early anthropological literature.

Nouveau riche. "Newly rich." People who have recently acquired wealth, typically those perceived as **ostentatious** or lacking in good taste by those with old inherited wealth.

Nuance. A subtle difference in meaning, physical expression or sound.

Numbers running. A formerly illegal form of daily lottery popular in urban communities. Runners would collect bets from local participants, and winners were paid based on selected "numbers." Often operated by organized crime groups before being replaced by state-run lotteries.

Numbing. Blocking feeling or responsiveness, through manipulation or a drug, to accomplish some goal that would have been difficult or impossible otherwise. Used in medical procedures but also by thieves and predators to disable victims.

Old suits. A term referring disparagingly to people with inherited wealth.

Ostentation. Showing off wealth and luxury to impress or attract attention.

Oxytocin. A hormone produced in the hypothalamus and released into the bloodstream by the pituitary gland. It is often called the "love hormone" because it induces a warm sense of affection and attraction. It can be stimulated by touch, or gestures of loving attention, and therefore can be manipulated to take advantage of others. (Also present especially during the process of giving birth.)

Palace guards. The defenders of power and privilege, including actual soldiers, a police force, media influencers or leaders of political and social institutions.
Parasite. An insect, animal or person who takes advantage of others, usually by numbing, hiding or deception.
Parasitic middleman. Someone who takes advantage of others simply by extracting fees from a transaction between other parties but without benefitting either.
Partisan. A strong supporter or defender of a party, cause, person or idea, often for historical or cultural reasons.
Passive resistance. Refusing to go along with an order, culture or force, but without using violence in the refusal.
Pathological. A physical or mental disease, or the intentional use of cruelty or other immoral means to accomplish a goal.
Pax Romana. Latin for "Roman peace." A period in Roman history, from 27 B.C.E. to 180 C.E., when the Roman Empire imposed stability on the lands under its control.
Pay differential. The difference in compensation between workers at various levels in a business.
People's art. Art created as propaganda during the early eras of communism and socialism. Also called "worker's art," depicting contented workers in fields and factories.
Philosophy. The study of wisdom, knowledge and reality, and its application to human life. Means literally "love of wisdom."
Political factions. A group with a common political purpose or ideology, especially one that has interests or opinions that vary from the majority of a political party.
Ponzi scheme. A fraud in which early investors are paid with money from later ones, creating an illusion of profit and legitimacy.
Predation. The attack of one animal or person on others who are considered "prey."
Predator. Among human beings, a person who exploits others.
Predatory hierarchy. The idea that among the many predators of the animal kingdom, there is a ranking from most powerful to least.
Predatory theft. Taking from a victim through deception or force.
Predestination. The idea that human life, and even all of nature, has its actions and future predetermined by God or the unchangeable mechanisms of physics and biology.
Profiteer. A person who makes a profit by taking advantage of others.
Propaganda. The use of words and actions to influence others, especially through lies or carefully crafted publicity, to manipulate them. A key technique of bullies in power.
Propagandist. Someone who creates or spreads propaganda in support of those in power, or seeking power.
Protection racket. A scheme where criminals demand payment for "protection" from threats they themselves pose. These payments are called "protection money" or "fees."
Psychology. The study of the human mind, especially in its behaviors in relationships or circumstances.
Purport. Claiming to be or do something, especially falsely.
Pyramid scheme. An illegal investment scam where returns to early participants are paid using money from new recruits. See also **Ponzi scheme**.

Racism. Prejudice, discrimination or antagonism toward a person or persons, based solely on their membership in a given ethnic group, usually a marginalized or a minority one.
Redistribution of wealth. The transfer of income, property or other assets from some people to others.
Redlining. Refusing a loan, insurance, business or other relations, to someone because they live in an area deemed to be a poor financial risk—usually because of poverty, social institutions or discrimination.
Redress of grievances. The right to ask the government to fix a wrong or provide compensation for it, protected by the First Amendment of the U.S. Constitution.
Regime. The leadership of a government, especially an **authoritarian** one.
Rhetoric. Originally meaning effective or persuasive speaking or writing, but also now implying speech intended to hide or deceive.
Rife. Common or widespread, especially of something harmful.
Roofie. To drug a person with flunitrazepam or a similar drug, usually hiding it in food or a drink, in order to rape, rob or otherwise victimize them.
Sacrilege. Violation, insult toward or misuse of something sacred, holy or important.
Sacrilegious. Committing sacrilege.
Scapegoat. A person who is blamed for the crimes, errors or faults of others.
Screed. A speech or piece of writing, typically regarded as tedious or hostile.
Seditious conspiracy. The crime of plotting against the government.
Seminal. Something that strongly influences later developments.
Septuagint. A Greek translation of the Hebrew Bible, made ~200 B.C.E. for Greek-speaking Jews in the Middle East. Includes additional books called the *Apocrypha*—texts not part of the Jewish canon but included in some Christian traditions.
Serf. An agricultural laborer bound under the **feudal** system to work on a large estate owned by someone else.
Sharecropping. The renting of a piece of landing by a farmer from a large landowner, giving a part of each crop as rent.
Shunning. To avoid, ignore or reject someone through dislike or distrust.
Skimming. Where someone, usually an employee, secretly steals a little bit of the goods or money, over time, but not enough to be noticed.
Slave. A person who is forced to work for another and is bound by force, law or social custom, so that they are not able to escape their circumstances.
Slipping a mickey. See **Mickey (slipping a)**.
Social gospel. Christian faith practiced as a call not just to personal faith, custom and worship but to social reform based on the teachings of Jesus to "love one another" and to "treat others the way you wish to be treated."
Socialism. A political and economic theory of social organization that advocates that the major means of production, distribution, and exchange should be owned or regulated by the community as a whole through elected or appointed officials.
Socialized medicine. A healthcare system where the government owns facilities, employs providers, and funds services through general taxes.
Sociology. The study of the structure and functioning of human societies.

Sovereign immunity. A legal doctrine that protects governments and rulers from being charged for civil or criminal wrongs.

Stoic. A member or advocate of the ancient philosophical school of **Stoicism**.

Stoicism. An ancient Greek school of philosophy founded at Athens by Zeno of Citium (~334–262 B.C.E.). It taught that virtue, grounded in knowledge, is the highest good, and that the wise live in harmony with divine Reason. Stoics aim to remain indifferent to pleasure, pain and fortune's changes.

Subjugation. To bring someone or something under domination or control.

Subsidy. Typically refers to a sum of money granted by the government or a public body to assist an industry or business to lower the price of a product or service.

Subsidize. To financially support an organization or activity.

Subvert. Undermine the power, authority or reputation of a system, institution or person.

Survival of the fittest. A concept propounded by Charles Darwin, from his observations of the persitent existence of organisms that are best-suited to their environmental challenges, with the extinction of others not so well-suited.

Tariff. A tax on imported or exported goods and services. Used to regulate trade, protect domestic industries and raise government revenue.

Totem. A natural object, artwork or animal believed by a culture to have spiritual significance or power, and that is adopted by it as an emblem or object of faith.

Trafficking. Deal or trade in something illegal, including goods, drugs and humans.

Treaty of Tordesillas. An agreement between Spain and Portugal in 1494 that divided the world into two spheres of influence. The treaty established a line of demarcation that separated the two kingdoms' claimed rights to own, discover, control and trade in the newly discovered lands outside of Europe.

Trepidation. A feeling of fear or anxiety about something that may happen.

Trust babies. People who inherited significant money or assets from a trust fund when they reached a certain age.

Tyrant. A cruel and oppressive ruler.

Ubiquitous. Found everywhere.

Unobtrusive. Present, but not conspicuous or attracting attention.

Utopia. A state in which everything is perfect or ideal.

Weaponization. Manipulating something such as existing laws, for the purpose of attacking a person or group, or for spreading distrust and discord.

Whistleblower. Someone who exposes a person or organization engaged in illicit or harmful activity.

White supremacist. A person who believes white people constitute a superior "race" and should therefore dominate society, to the detriment of other ethnic groups.

Witch burnings. The act of burning to death people accused of witchcraft. This was a common form of execution during the European and American witch-hunts that took place between the 14th and 18th centuries.

INDEX

A Brief Account of the Destruction of the Indies, 69
abundance, 3, 4, 10, 29, 35, 81, 100, 102, 105, 117, 118, 119, 135, 136, 138, 139, 140, 153, 161, 162, 164
abuse, 3, 22, 23, 47, 77, 165
Affordable Care Act, 80
Africa, 29, 37, 38, 44, 69, 70, 71, 73, 95, 101, 132, 146, 169
Agnostic, 167
Alexander the Great, 29, 31, 33, 34, 65, 66, 171
Aliens, 169
Anarchy, 167
apex, 9, 15, 20, 29, 32, 35, 56, 139, 161
apex predator, 9, 20, 95, 161
Apex Predator, 167
Apologetics, 167
Apostasy, 167
Appalachia, 72
Aquinas, Thomas, 30
Aristotle, 30, 66, 67, 71, 73, 111
Aryan, 167
Asia, 169
authoritarian, 144, 167, 175
authority, 141
authority, expert, 142, 143, 147
authority, granted, 147
authority, imposed, 144, 145
authority, ingrained, 145
authority, overthrown and replaced, 145, 146
authority, persistent, 144
Autocrat/Autocratic, 167
Aztec, 167
Baha'i Faith, 107
Bartolome de las Casas, 69
Big Pharma, 169
Blacklists, 168
Blasphemy, 86, 168
Bloody Sunday, 58
Bolshevik, 58, 168
bourgeoisie, 168
bribery, 23, 26, 27, 28, 121, 169
Bribery, 168
British Empire, 101
Buddhism, 107
bullies, i, v, vii, 3, 4, 5, 6, 7, 9, 10, 13, 15, 16, 17, 18, 20, 21, 22, 23, 24, 25, 27, 28, 29, 31, 32, 33, 34, 35, 36, 37, 38, 39, 41, 48, 53, 54, 55, 56, 57, 59, 60, 61, 62, 63, 64, 65, 66, 69, 71, 75, 77, 81, 82, 83, 84, 86, 87, 88, 89, 90, 91, 97, 100, 101,103, 110, 111, 117, 118, 119, 121, 131, 133, 134, 135, 138, 139, 140, 141, 144, 145, 146, 147, 148, 150, 152, 159, 161, 163, 164, 165

bully, 16, 17, 18, 19, 20, 21, 23, 25, 26, 33, 34, 36, 38, 41, 53, 56, 60, 62, 77, 101, 135, 139, 146, 147, 157, 162
Caesar Augustus, 31
capitalism, 3, 57, 59, 82, 146, 151, 152, 168
Cartel, 168
Castro, 168
Cat-fisher, 168
Central America, 169
Christianity, 107, 167
Civil Rights Act, 102
Civil Rights Movement, 97
Civil War, 38, 96, 101
Clarkson, Thomas, 101
Class Warfare, 168, 169
coal mines, 72, 73
Cold War, 19, 168
Collateral damage, 168
communism, 18, 19, 56, 57, 58, 60, 61, 76, 138, 146, 152, 169
communist, 18, 19, 21, 81, 82, 98
Communist Party, 168
Community Action Project (CAP), 97, 98, 100
con man, 169
Confucianism, 107
conning, 42, 53, 54, 84, 85, 169
conquerors, 6, 37, 39, 77, 133, 162
conquest, iii, 3, 18, 31, 32, 37, 60, 63, 68, 135, 171, 173
Conquistador, 169
conspiracy, 42, 48, 49, 52, 61, 82, 84, 86, 87, 169, 175
conspiracy theories, 52, 86, 169
Conversion, 49, 169
corruption, 6, 22, 23, 25, 27, 28, 121, 169
cults, 25, 52, 85, 86, 138
Das Kapital, 18
deceit, 7, 19, 41, 75
Deep State, 169
democracy, 60, 133, 149, 150, 152
depravity, 16
despair, 80
Despots, 169
discrimination, 54, 175
distraction, 37, 42, 49, 52, 89
divine right of kings, 58, 69, 132, 144
economic systems, 6, 7, 60, 63, 81, 82, 150, 151, 152, 164, 168
economic systems, Communism, 151
economic systems, Feudalism, 150, 171
economic systems, Hunter-Gatherer, 150
economic systems, Socialism, 150
economic systems, Capitalism, 151
Egypt, 167
Ehrlichman, John, 22

177

Elders of Zion, 169
Emancipation Proclamation, 64, 102, 170
embezzlement, 42, 49, 55
Engels, 168
Enlightenment, 170
entitlement, 56, 76
eugenics, 95
European Lottery, 51
Evil Laws, 42, 54
exploit, 3, 7, 60, 63, 100, 152
exploitation, 3, 4, 6, 35, 63, 101, 103, 131, 135, 137, 155, 162, 163, 164, 171
extortion, 27, 47
false authority, 87
fraud, 121, 138, 142, 143
freedom, 4, 6, 21, 68, 73, 86, 111, 117, 132, 134, 140, 141, 164, 170, 173
gangs, 3, 23, 25, 26
Genghis Khan, 31, 32, 33, 34, 65
genocide, 60, 69
Ghandi, 39
gladiators, 67
Golden Circle, 85
harm, 6, 13, 15, 16, 26, 36, 48, 62, 63, 65, 89, 103
health insurance, 75, 124, 125
healthcare, 9, 57, 59, 76, 81, 105, 119, 122, 123, 124, 125, 126, 127, 128, 129, 131, 138, 139, 152, 155, 158, 163
hierarchy, 24, 55, 59, 64, 158, 174
Hinduism, 107
Hitler, Adolph, 34, 60
Holocaust, the, 59
Hoover, J. Edgar, 19, 21
House Unamerican Activities Committee (HUAC), 19
human trafficking, 74
Humanism, 171
Illuminati, 169
immigrants, 72, 74, 75, 81
immigration, 74
indigenous, 33, 69, 132, 167
intimidation, 89
Islam, 107
Jainism, 108
Jefferson, Thomas, 71
Judaism, 108
King, Martin Luther, Jr., 39, 97
Koch, George August, i
Lenin, Vladimir, 18, 59
lies, 3, 5, 7, 11, 15, 19, 20, 21, 22, 26, 38, 41, 47, 50, 51, 55, 56, 57, 61, 62, 69, 76, 77, 82, 83, 84, 87, 88, 89, 102, 117, 119, 139, 142, 143, 152
love, ii, 3, 4, 11, 34, 35, 48, 62, 98, 99, 100, 104, 137
loving, 99, 100, 105, 107, 118, 119, 148, 166
Maimonides, 30

Mao Zedong, 18, 34, 56, 168
Marcus Aurelius, 71
mark, 46, 53, 54, 85
Marx, Karl, 18, 56, 57, 168
Marxism, 56, 61, 76, 81, 169
McCarthy, Senator Joe, 19
Mexico, 169
middle class, 56, 63, 64, 75, 80
minimum wage, 54, 75, 80
miscegenation, 96
misdirection, 7, 41, 42, 45, 47, 52, 55, 76, 77, 149, 173
mob, 23, 24, 25, 26, 83
moral, 24, 25, 26, 29, 33, 38, 60, 65, 74, 76, 82, 87, 96, 100, 107, 153, 155, 158, 165
Multi-Level Marketing, 173
Multi-Level-Marketing (MLM), 85
mutual care, 3, 4, 7, 9, 10, 13, 26, 29, 32, 34, 35, 39, 46, 53, 56, 60, 61, 81, 82, 87, 90, 97, 100, 102, 103, 105, 107, 109, 110, 117, 118, 119, 121, 127, 128, 131, 135, 136, 137, 138, 139, 140, 143, 146, 147, 148, 149, 152, 153, 155, 156, 157, 161, 162, 163, 164
NAACP, 97, 98, 173
Native American Spirituality, 108
Nazis, 24, 167
negroes, 96, 97
Nixon, Richard, 22
North Vietnam, 168
numbing, 42, 47, 48, 89, 91, 173
Oceana, 169
Octavian, 30, 31
October Revolution of 1917, 168
opposition, 18, 21, 22, 60, 61, 86, 157
oppression, 28, 56, 72, 73, 74, 90, 134, 144
Palace guards, 89, 90, 174
parasites, 3, 4, 5, 7, 13, 25, 27, 29, 31, 33, 34, 39, 41, 42, 45, 46, 47, 49, 50, 51, 53, 54, 55, 56, 57, 59, 61, 63, 64, 65, 66, 69, 75, 76, 77, 81, 82, 83, 85, 86, 87, 88, 89, 90, 97, 100, 101, 103, 111, 117, 119, 121, 131, 133, 134, 135, 138, 139, 140, 141, 143, 144, 146, 147, 148, 150, 152, 163, 164
Pax Romana, 31, 174
peace, 16, 17, 31, 105, 118, 136, 174
Ponzi scheme, 59, 85, 174
Ponzi Scheme, 173
Poor leaders, 157
Portuguese s, 169
poverty, 3, 64, 72, 73, 74, 78, 79, 80, 81, 82, 119, 140, 152
power, 3, 5, 6, 7, 9, 18, 20, 21, 22, 23, 25, 27, 31, 32, 33, 34, 35, 36, 48, 49, 52, 53, 54, 55, 56, 58, 59, 60, 61, 62, 64, 65, 67, 68, 75, 77, 83, 88, 89, 91, 97, 101, 117, 131, 132, 133, 138, 146, 161, 169, 170, 176

predator, 6, 9, 10, 15, 20, 26, 32, 39, 41, 56, 90, 139, 146, 161, 167
predatory hierarchy, 141
prejudice, 96
privilege, 3, 5, 6, 18, 23, 34, 53, 56, 74, 84, 96, 138, 145, 174
proletariat, 168
propaganda, 15, 18, 25, 32, 41, 55, 57, 59, 62, 76, 81, 83, 84, 86, 87, 88, 89, 90, 91, 115, 123, 138, 149, 168, 174
protection rackets, 23
proxy wars, 168
racism, 54, 95, 111
Ranavalona, 33, 34, 38, 65
redistribution of wealth, 56, 76
red-lining, 97, 111
resistance, 16, 39, 89, 134
rights, basic, 131, 132
ruling class, 168
Russian Social Democratic Party, 168
sacrifice, 26, 35, 39, 60, 90
scamming, 44, 51, 84, 85
seditious conspiracy, 48
Sharp, Granville, 101
Sikhism, 108
skimming, 42, 43, 44, 49, 175
slavery, 29, 34, 38, 63, 64, 65, 66, 67, 68, 69, 70, 71, 72, 73, 74, 76, 77, 81, 82, 101, 111, 139
slaves, 3, 5, 7, 13, 25, 27, 28, 31, 32, 33, 46, 57, 59, 63, 64, 65, 66, 67, 68, 69, 71, 73, 75, 76, 77, 81, 87, 102, 117, 119, 131, 132, 133, 139, 141, 144, 148, 150, 152, 163
socialism, 56, 57, 59, 61, 76, 117, 138, 146, 150, 152, 175
socialist, 81, 125, 151, 169
socialized medicine, 57
Society for the Abolition of the Slave Trade, 38
South America, 169
South Vietnam, 168
sovereign immunity, 133
Spanish conquerors, 169
Spartacus, 67, 73, 132, 145
Stalin, Joseph, 18, 34, 59, 60, 168
stealing, 3, 4, 6, 7, 13, 15, 16, 17, 23, 24, 29, 32, 37, 39, 41, 43, 45, 46, 47, 48, 49, 50, 51, 52, 55, 57, 65, 68, 86, 90, 100, 103, 119, 121
Stoics, 66, 176

stolen, 15, 36, 37, 45, 50, 56, 67, 79, 143, 145
subjugation, 33
subsidizing, 3, 23, 25, 26, 53, 57, 61, 64, 71, 73, 74, 77, 81, 82, 83, 87, 100, 133, 138, 139, 163, 176
supervision, good, 155, 156, 157, 158
survival of the fittest, 9, 140
Taoism, 108
taxes, 54, 88, 121, 122
The Communist Manifesto, 18
The Declaration of Independence (United States, July 4, 1776), 132
The Declaration of the Rights of Man (France, 1789), 132
The Golden Rule, 107, 109, 135, 163
The Indies, 68, 69
The Magna Carta (England 1215), 132
theft, 6, 13, 15, 24, 26, 27, 36, 41, 43, 44, 45, 46, 49, 50, 51, 52, 53, 54, 56, 63, 67, 91, 103, 121, 123, 126, 131, 138, 143, 172, 174
thieves, 13, 36, 37, 41, 42, 46, 75, 77, 100, 105, 122
threaten, 16, 62, 86, 141, 159
tolls, 28
Treaty of Tordesillas, 68, 176
tyranny, 146
tyrants, 36, 37, 131
unalienable rights, 133, 134, 135, 147
Unitarianism, 108
universal healthcare, 128
victim, 9, 11, 15, 16, 28, 31, 37, 41, 46, 53, 54, 63, 70, 76, 85, 161
victimhood, 23, 46
victimize, 3, 32, 175
Vietnam, 18, 19
violence, 6, 9, 15, 20, 39, 83, 86, 145
Washington, George, 71
weaponization, 22, 176
well-being, 38, 54, 55, 105, 140, 161
white flight, 97
Who Think Alone Grow Peculiar, 165
Wilberforce, William, 38, 101
wisdom, 66, 100, 103, 104, 105, 107, 118, 119, 122, 148, 156
workers, 168
working poor, 64, 76, 85
worldview, 24, 25, 86
Yoruba, 108

www.ingramcontent.com/pod-product-compliance
Lightning Source LLC
Chambersburg PA
CBHW061140230426
43663CB00027B/2982